What others are saying about Shannon Perry's
THE OVERLOOKED GENERATION

Combining informative information with scriptural principles, Shannon Perry offers parents practical, yet timeless advice on how to raise teens and tweens in an ever-evolving culture.

–**Josh McDowell,** *popular speaker,*
author and co-author of 138 books,
including New Evidence That Demands a Verdict,
recognized as one of the top 40 books of the 20th Century.
Josh McDowell Ministry is a division of Campus Crusade
for Christ International.

"Informative, insightful, and inspirational, *The Overlooked Generation* is a "must read" for all parents, grandparents, and anyone else who interacts regularly with "teens and tweens." The suggestions are supported by timeless Scripture references, making this book an indispensable tool at our counseling center."

–**Dr. Eriko Valk,** *Psychologist/CEO Liberty Path, Inc.*

"Through my career as a counselor I've been fortunate to work with thousands of tweens and teens. Shannon Perry's book *The Overlooked Generation* equips parents with a vital tool of practical, realistic, scripture-based insight to aid them in the tough task of building their children's foundation. I implore parents to put Shannon's guidance into practice. They need you parents, more than you ever know."

–**Megan McC....** *M...... ....*
Licensed P...

D1115528

"*The Overlooked Generation* is a must have for parents raising teenagers. In this book, Shannon Perry gives practical advice that parents can use to tackle the common, as well as tough issues with their teens. Shannon's background as a school counselor gives her insight to the tools that have been tested and tried in the school setting and crucial in the home. The idea of setting boundaries and being a role model are two of the most profound suggestions in the book. This book is a great hands-on tool for parents raising teenagers, and I know that everyone who reads this book will be blessed by the wisdom Shannon shares."

–Dr. Lisa Henderson Hubbard, *Doctorate in Urban Education/Masters of Education/Counseling*

"In *The Overlooked Generation*, Shannon Perry speaks to important issues that parents face as they raise their children. Shannon loves her Lord and Savior, loves people and is passionate about helping young people and their parents. She gives attention to the truth you and your children need to hear in a world that screams so many lies. You will gain valuable information and Biblical insight on how God wants us to live. My church had the opportunity to host an "In Her Shoes" event where Shannon led mothers and daughters speaking to the very issues that are included in this book. Mothers and daughters alike were challenged, inspired and encouraged!"

–Rhonda Mohr, *Family Life Minister*

"Shannon Perry's, *The Overlooked Generation*, is an informative book every parent should read to understand the devastating effects of bullying and what steps can be taken to alleviate it."

–Rebecca Roberts, B.Ed., *Classroom Teacher, 30 years' experience*

THE
OVERLOOKED
GENERATION

THE
OVERLOOKED
GENERATION

Parenting Teens and Tweens
in a Complicated Culture

SHANNON PERRY

The Overlooked Generation - Parenting Teens and Tweens in a Complicated Culture
©2013 by Shannon Perry

Published in Franklin, Tennessee, by Carpenter's Son Publishing, in association with Larry Carpenter of Christian Book Services, LLC www.christianbookservices.com

Cover design by Mia Stojanovic.

ISBN-13: 978-0-9893722-4-4

Printed in the United States of America.

For resources and speaking information:
www.ShannonPerry.com, or write to Chae Music,
P.O. Box 2887, Cypress, TX 77410-2887

OVERLOOK:

a. Fail to notice

b. Ignore or Disregard

Acknowledgements

THE Author and Finisher of my faith – thank you, Jesus, for the eternal certainty that we are never "overlooked."

Mom – We traveled many miles as this book was born. I love you more than I can put into words.

Dad – Your example of unconditional love is a mirror of God's love for his kids. You ARE "good"… "I know it"…and I love you so much.

Gina – Your constant encouragement, powerful reminders and wise insights are treasures in my life. Your sense of humor is the treasure box.

Sarah – Your tireless efforts to get the job done are incredible. Thank you for serving alongside me and for loving me along the way. I'm so proud of you.

Laurie – Your unending dedication to serve amazes me. Thank you for preparing every detail of this book with excellence.

Leah – Your friendship is priceless. Thanks for allowing me to use your insight in the book – you are a mom that all should emulate. Love you more.

Jennifer – Thank you for your help with research, for sharing ideas and for the great example you are as a mom.

Holly – Your strength will forever amaze me and your beautiful heart will forever amaze us all.

Sean and Michelle – I love you and thank God every day for blessing my life with you.

David – Thank you for being the one to suggest I go into ministry and for recognizing gifts I never knew I possessed. I love you.

Josh McDowell – For being one of the first to teach me that God's Word works in every area of life. Your ministry is life-changing.

TABLE OF CONTENTS

"OVERLOOKED"

©2013 Paul Marino and Shannon Perry

We all have the same fears
We all cry the same tears
We all have anxieties
And awkward insecurities
We all have the same hopes
And we all have the same dreams
We all have the same need to be loved

Chorus:
No one likes to be the last one chosen for the team
Always a bridesmaid never a bride
What it's like to be forgotten and misunderstood
If you find someone like that let them know
They're not overlooked

We all know the hurt that comes
From being shamed or being shunned
When all is said and all is done
We've all felt that way

Chorus:
No one likes to be the last one chosen for the team
Always a bridesmaid never a bride
What it's like to be forgotten and misunderstood
If you find someone like that let them know
They're not overlooked

PROLOGUE

"Train up a child in the way he should go: and when he is old, he will not depart from it."

Proverbs 22:6

Before I began traveling the country teaching and singing at women's events, I worked with teens in a variety of settings. By the age of twenty one, I was deemed Staff Director of a Christian Camp which mentored over four thousand teens each summer. Our goal was to teach teens the truth from God's Word and how to practically apply His Word to the different scenarios they would face throughout their teenage years.

As a public school teacher and school counselor for fourteen years, I had the opportunity to not only hear the issues that parents and teens face, but to witness the outcomes that occurred as a result of the counsel I offered. God has allowed me the unique opportunity once again of working with teens through my latest conference for moms and daughters, "In Her Shoes." The questions and concerns brought to me by both moms and daughters during "In Her Shoes" are the driving force behind this book. As parents reached out for help with the difficult situations they faced, two things became obvious: 1.) parents want practical ideas and tips and, 2.) our teens are desperately trying to fill a void in their life. Some will go to any degree to fill the void, but where did it come from?

I believe God showed me the answer to that question in one word: "overlooked." Many of our teens feel overlooked, and they are searching for answers everywhere. Our job as parents is to let them know they are not overlooked as we teach them the TRUTH of God's Word about His love for them. My prayer for you as you read this book is that you would find "real" answers to "real" problems in a "real" guide-book – God's Word. While there is great research on the subject of parenting a teen, the best and most practical advice we can receive is from the Bible.

Whatever you and your teen may be experiencing, know you are not alone. Throughout the book I have made reference to real-life stories to remind you that others have faced similar issues. Names have been changed to protect those involved, but the issues are real and so are the outcomes.

As you apply the truth of God's Word and the suggestions of this book, may you continually be reminded that you and your teen are never "overlooked" by our Heavenly Father. He will gently guide you to be the parent He designed you to be as you make a powerful impact in this "overlooked generation."

CHAPTER ONE

HONOR THE MAMA!

"Making the decision to have a child is momentous. It is to decide forever to have your heart go walking around outside your body."

-Elizabeth Stone

From the time I was born, my parents took me to church. I have great memories of church events, but two particular moments stand out above the others.

The first is the night I walked the aisle and asked Jesus Christ to come into my heart when I was six years old. "The Cruise Family" had come to sing at my church and Cindy Cruise took me aboard their tour bus. I knew instantly that I wanted to be a singer, and God allowed the dream of a little girl's heart to become a reality. Fortunately, He blessed me with a love for talking as well, and I have been doing so ever since. I often joke, "What they used to put me in the corner for doing when I was in school, they are now paying me to do." God has such amazing plans for us even when we are young.

I also remember the night I got sick in church. It was one of the most embarrassing nights of my church-going life, but one that brought me to a deep, theological understanding - "HONOR THE MAMA!"

Before a Wednesday night church service, I decided that brownies were what was for dinner.

The problem came when I lied to my mom about the brownies. She warned me several times that I could have one brownie (not the entire package) after I ate the dinner she prepared. When she left the room, I tucked the brownies into my coat and digested eight of the delectable pastries before going into church.

As the choir began singing "How Great Thou Art," I remember thinking, "How great I'm not." Suddenly, and with a thunderous upheaval, I emptied my brownies all over the lady in the pew in front of me. The entire church service came to a halt and the truth had been revealed. I had dishonored my mama.

The truth always has a way of suddenly and thunderously showing up. God's Word reminds us that the truth always shines in the darkness, and that the truth will set us free (John 8:32).

God commands children to honor their parents in the Ten Commandments "that their days may be long upon the earth."

You may be thinking, "My kid has one good day left if that verse is true." Remember that the truth will set you AND your child free to live the life that God designed for you.

I remember when truth set one of my students and her mother free. I was counseling a fifth grader named Beth who was a "cutter" and was hiding her pain from her family. The more I spoke with Beth, the more I realized that the pain she was inflicting on herself was aimed directly at her mother. The mom was favoring the sister in the family and refused to give Beth the attention she desperately desired. Beth was feeling overlooked. I called the mom into my office and disclosed my concerns. She was horrified to learn that Beth was cutting, but refused to recognize her contribution to the problem. After several counseling sessions, Beth's mom was able to see a pattern, and realized she had the power to help with Beth's problem. Beth and her mom worked with me for a year. Their relationship grew and eventually, Beth stopped cutting. Healing came as a result of Beth and her mom facing truth in a difficult situation.

So how do we implement truth in our lives and the lives of our children? We do what the Bible tells us to do.

When we begin to believe anything other than what the Bible says, we begin to believe half-truths or lies. As you are well aware, there are many things in the world today which try to tell our kids what "truth" is. From technology to pop culture and peers, "truth" comes in all shapes and sizes. No wonder our kids are confused! They are dealing with a greater influx of information than any generation has ever encountered. According to research, our teens have more information available to them in one day than the former generations had available throughout their entire childhood ("How Technology is Influencing Families").

So, how can we know as parents that the truth of God's Word works? We will know it works when we implement it in our own lives. We can trust God to work in our lives, and the lives of our children, when we do life His way. Remember, if we want something to be important in our kid's lives, we must make it important in our lives. When we model the behavior that we desire for our kids, the truth becomes the standard in our home.

Remember, if we want something to be important in our kid's lives, we must make it important in our lives.

If you long for your kids to honor you as the parent, then live obediently to your Heavenly Father. When we honor God, we set a wonderful example for our teens to follow and implement in their own lives.

PARENT PAUSE:

1. What is your idea of receiving honor from your child? What does that look like?

2. How will you effectively speak God's Word into the life of your child so that it is applicable, relevant and timely?

3. Are there some areas where you long to make the truth of God's Word more relevant in your own life?

CHAPTER TWO

YOU'RE WEARING THAT?

"The best part of beauty is that which no picture can express."

-*Francis Bacon*

One of the most common questions I receive from parents is, "What can I do about the way my child dresses?" Ironically, one of the most common questions I receive from teens is, "Why do my parents make such a big deal about the way I dress?"

Throughout time, parents and teens have differed on style. I'm sure you can remember when you knew how cute you were, only to learn that your parents found nothing cute about your wardrobe. I certainly can.

Every night, my daddy would sit in his big black chair in the living room. It was impossible to get to the front door of the house without walking by him, so he had every opportunity to rate my wardrobe before I left home. Most nights, I scored well. Some nights, however, he never spoke a word. He would shake his head "no" and point back to my room. I knew that meant one thing – "You're not wearing THAT anywhere."

I remember one incident I still find humorous. In the late eighties, it was popular to wear men's boxer shorts over sweatpants (I'm still trying to grasp how we thought this looked good). I will never forget my dad asking me, "Why are you wearing men's underwear out in public?" It struck me as funny and I knew he was right (although I would have never admitted it). But I wasn't thinking about how silly it was. I only knew that everyone else was wearing them and I didn't want to be different.

Perhaps you are fighting the "everyone else is wearing it" battle. Clothes are usually part of the hunt when kids are searching for identity and they place great importance on looking good. The same child you used to beg to take a bath now spends hours in the bathroom just looking at themselves. As teens grow, they become more and more consumed with appearance - theirs and others.

With technology at the fingertips of every teenager, it doesn't take long for a style to gain popularity. If our teen is not wearing it, they often feel left out, shunned and overlooked. Magazines, television, the internet, YouTube, and many other media outlets send one message: "You must look a certain way and wear a certain thing to fit in and be popular."

Culture has pressured us as parents AND teens to dress in certain ways. A study by the American

Psychological Association found that after three minutes of looking at fashion magazines, 70% of women (moms and daughters) said they felt "depressed, guilty, and ashamed" about how they looked. Why? Because we have allowed the media to dictate what "pretty" looks like, and we compare ourselves to the models they present. Do you know what I like to do with some of those magazines when I'm standing in line at the grocery store? I TURN THEM OVER. The images on those magazines may be attractive, but I can assure you, those models are not flawless in REAL life. They have been airbrushed and touched up to look a certain way so that we buy into the lie that "perfection" is the mark we must achieve. When we base the way we feel about ourselves on what the media is saying we're in trouble because none of us will ever attain perfection.

The media also enjoys shock value through their "sex sells" campaigns. Just step into a shopping mall and it won't take long to see ads of teenagers wearing things that would have been considered R-rated twenty years ago. Should we just accept that sexual obsession is the new norm and that we as parents will have to adjust? Hardly.

Because sexual images are so prevalent in our society, it is more important than ever to spend time talking with our kids about the images they see in the media. Talk with your teen about the culture's sexually-explicit messages, and how they contrast with your family's values. While there is nothing wrong with striving to look fashionable, there is a big difference between looking pretty and looking provocative.

Remember that most teens dress to gain attention and that some may not fully understand the difference between positive and negative attention. This is where we as parents play a critical role. We must model clothes that are age-appropriate in front of our children. Moms, if we want our daughters to dress in ways that attract positive attention, we must do the same. If there is a part of our body showing that only a husband should see, we need to cover it up. The same applies for husbands. When we get dressed, it is healthy to give ourselves a "double-take" before we walk out the door. Are we wearing a shirt that's revealing, shorts not made for kneeling or pants that look like peeling? If so, give it a second thought. As parents, it is healthy to look our best and we should STRIVE to look our best. We can still "paint the barn," but our teen needs someone who loves them enough to set the example, or mainstream media will do it for us.

God's Word also has a lot to say about the way we dress. I Timothy 2:9-10 says that God wants women (and young ladies) to be modest in their appearance. We should wear appropriate clothing because those who are devoted to God "make themselves look good by the good things they do."

Leviticus 11:44 also reminds us that we must be holy, for He is holy. That includes the way we dress. We can be cute and classy as we live right in the middle of a holy life. Assure your teen that you are not trying to be insulting about their clothes, but that you want him/her to view themselves respectfully. Many girls, for example, are known to dress in certain ways because they believe it will be more attractive to guys.

Research shows that guys are INITIALLY attracted to girls who are dressed more provocatively, but that the attraction doesn't last ("Modesty Survey"). During my Mother/Daughter conference "In Her Shoes," I show a video of three guys having a conversation as they discuss four different girls and the way they are dressed. While the guys readily admit they are initially attracted to the more provocatively dressed girl, they ALL say that they would not have a long term relationship with her. Why? Because they could not respect a girl who disrespects herself by the way she dresses. They go on to say that they would not have a serious relationship with the provocatively dressed girl because they fear she is hiding deeper issues behind her need for attention.

If a girl wants a guy to respect her, she must respect herself by the way she dresses. If a guy wants to find a girl that is worthy of respect, he can draw a conclusion by the way she dresses. Romans 14:13 tells us that we must live in such a way that we do not put a stumbling block in another Christian's path. We can help one another in this area just by the way we dress. A good slogan to remember is, "Think classy, not trashy." Not only will it help us when we are making clothing selections, but it will help us in securing the "right" kind of attention. I know this to be true in my own life.

My husband David has often said, "What attracted me to you is the way you dressed and carried yourself. You dressed classy and carried yourself with confidence." Remember, class is not about money. Class is about self-respect, and the way we honor others by our behavior. When we are out in the world, it is possible for others to look at us and know we are Christians by our actions – including the way we dress. I Peter 2:9 says, "You are a chosen people...God has called you out of darkness and into His marvelous light." Our bodies are a "temple of the Holy Spirit" according to I Corinthians 6:19, and when we honor God by the way we dress, our bodies do not stand out as the focus to others, our hearts do.

While some teens are conservative in dress, others are not. How can we as parents respond if our teen dresses inappropriately? While we are not physically

Parents, we have the final say.

dressing our children as teens, they are still considered minors by law until they are eighteen years of age. As parents, we have a responsibility to care for them in every way, including the way that they dress. Parents, we have the final say. While the teen should always have input into what they wear, the final decision is our responsibility because God has entrusted them to our care.

If you are facing conflict in the area of appearance, talk with your teen about the kind of clothes they feel best express their individuality. Encourage your teen to go shopping with you and find clothes you can both agree on. Remind your teen girl, for example, that if cleavage is showing when she tries on a shirt, it's too low. Tank tops under shirts are always helpful and spandex shorts under a shorter skirt are a good alternative. Remember, most school systems reinforce the rule that if the middle finger tip does not reach the bottom of a pair of shorts on your teen, they're too short. No one wants to see bellies, behinds, or bras.

While boys do not often present the same challenges in the wardrobe department, there is one exception – keep your drawers up! There is nothing more unflattering than the crotch of a boy's pants that drags the ground. No one wants to see Mickey Mouse boxer shorts hanging out of our teen's pants or his seat dragging the floor. This is also unacceptable in many public facilities.

When I was a school counselor, "droopy drawers" were not acceptable by our school policy. One of my students had been warned numerous times that he should be wearing a belt to school, but unfortunately, he continually forgot. Phone calls were made home as a reminder, and one day I had the duty of making the call. His mom said, in no uncertain terms, "I have told that boy to wear a belt I don't know how many times. I can't leave my job to come up to that school, so staple his belt loops together if you have to." With permission, we did exactly as the mom requested. Bobby walked the school halls all day with his belt loops stapled together, and to my knowledge, he never forgot his belt again. When teen boys enter a court-house or school yard, they are often dismissed from the grounds if they cannot find a way to wear their pants more appropriately.

As we give our teens the opportunity to choose what they wear, we must remind them that we will support their choices as long as their outfits don't go against God's Word or put them in danger. When we allow our teen to state their identity by choosing what to wear, we show them we believe they can be trusted to make good decisions. If the clothes go against the standards listed above, don't be afraid of conflict. Coming to an agreement you can both adhere to is a healthy compromise.

When we have a teen that is unwilling to cooperate in the wardrobe department, there are a few things we can do. First, we must gently remind our teen that it is a "normal" part of the parent-child relationship to see things differently. If your teen refuses to compromise with you and continues to dress in ways that are inappropriate, you must draw stronger boundaries. Remember, YOU are the parent and God has given you the privilege, as well as the responsibility, to guide your child. Too many times, parents are intimidated by teen's threats when they don't get their way. DO NOT let your child manipulate you. When your child finds that they can manipulate you in the smaller areas, such as dress, it will get worse when you are facing larger decisions.

If your teen refuses to obey your dress code standards, enforce healthy boundaries. First of all, monitor what your teen buys at the store. Typically, it is your money and your teen must know that as long as you are paying for the clothes, you will need to approve of them. If your teen is using money they earn from an allowance, let them know they will not continue to earn money if the reasonable guidelines you have set are not followed. If your teen buys something inappropriate while out shopping with friends, you can help them make a better choice when you accompany them to return their inappropriate purchase.

If your child has a job and is earning money, but lives under your roof, you still have the responsibility to monitor their wardrobe. I know parents who have gone so far as to clean their children's closets when they were away from home and left only those clothes that are age-appropriate. While this may seem extreme to some, teens that refuse to respect boundaries need tough consequences. Setting boundaries is part of showing your child love.

What do we do if our teens have been prohibited to wear certain clothing and they change outfits once they leave the house? There are several things you may need to do if this is the case. Initially, discuss your concerns with your teen. Let him/her know why you are concerned about the kind of clothes they are wearing once they leave home. Remind them that you have safety concerns and apply real-life principles. For example, the clothes that land them in the principal's office now may get them fired from their job in later years.

If your teen continues to disobey your request, you may need to set stronger boundaries. Accompanying your teen to all their activities is always an option. I can almost guarantee that once you offer this suggestion, your teen will more than likely be quick to abide by your request.

Part of parenting this "overlooked generation" is being creative. Use technology to your advantage. Have your teen text full pictures of themselves to you throughout the night while they are out with friends. Do not let your teen know the times that you will be requesting the text, or they will be able to change clothes ahead of time. While this may sound extreme, I speak from experience. Not only will you be able to see what they are wearing, but your teen will quickly tire of changing clothes each time you make a request. If they refuse to abide by your request, they may need to remain at home for a period of time to think about how they can respect your request. Remember, trust is earned.

Remember, trust is earned.

As you go through this process, remember to choose your battles. If the clothes your child is wearing do not go against Godly standards or put your child at risk, ask yourself if it is worth the battle. If they want to wear UGG® slippers to the mall in the middle of July, is it worth the battle?

Reminding our kids that there are appropriate ways to dress for different occasions is also important. We don't go ice skating in a wedding dress and we don't go to a wedding in a tennis skirt. Too many times, our kids have lost the desire to look nice simply because "casual" has become the norm. There are some situations that require our teen to dress more formally, and we can guide them by educating them on the difference.

A sense of humor is important when it comes to discussing delicate topics with our teens. Model a piece of clothing that is outrageous and ask your teen if they would be embarrassed to be seen with you dressed in such a way. If they say no, offer to wear that bright orange plaid the next time they have friends over. You may find they will quickly change their mind about your funky wardrobe, and get the point. Just as they don't want to be embarrassed by the way you are dressed, neither are you willing to be embarrassed by the way they dress.

As parents, we can get angry with the clothing companies who use ads to sell inappropriate clothing, but if we will stop supporting them, we can send a powerful message. Our teens deserve to be sold clothing that helps them find self-respect, and ultimately, money talks. When we refuse to buy clothes for our teens that are inappropriate, the clothing market WILL take notice.

When talking with your teen about the way they dress, be sure to put the emphasis on the fact that they are more than what they wear. Clothes don't make the person. It's who we are in Christ and the heart that shines from beneath the clothes that set us apart.

PARENT PAUSE:

1. Is there an area in your teen's wardrobe that needs to be addressed? If so, what is the best way to approach your teen?
2. How can you help remind your teen of the value and identity they have apart from what they wear?
3. Are there any areas in your wardrobe that might need altering in order to live a more holy life?

CHAPTER THREE

DYING TO BE THIN

"My worst days in recovery are better than the best days in relapse."

-Kate Le Page

I sat silently as I listened to the voice on the other end of the phone. "Mrs. Perry, I don't know what to do." Through tears, a mom told me her daughter was sitting in a downtown hospital being treated for an eating disorder and begged me to go visit. Ashley was a beautiful, sixteen year old scholarship recipient to some of the highest-ranking universities in the country. Unfortunately, the mirror in her mind did not reflect what the rest of the world saw, and she began to binge and purge in order to meet the culture's criteria for "beautiful."

Too many times I have visited hospital rooms where teens are starving themselves to overcome the lies which scream, "You are not enough." There are two major eating disorders most often recognized and they are life stealers.

Anorexia nervosa is the extreme obsession and fear of

gaining weight. Bulimia is also the fear of gaining weight, but is controlled differently from anorexia.

Anorexia is an addiction just like alcoholism and drug use. The body produces tremendous amounts of adrenaline when the body's blood sugar drops to low levels and the anorexic becomes addicted to the adrenaline. Just as any addiction, dealing with anorexia or bulimia can be very lonely and isolating for victims and their families.

To recognize the symptoms of anorexia or bulimia, we must be able to identify the characteristics associated with each.

To be diagnosed with anorexia, the following must be present in our teen:

* Refusal to maintain body weight at or above a minimally normal weight range for age and height

* An intense fear of being fat although they are obviously underweight

* Have a distorted view of their body or deny that their low weight is a problem

* Have amenorrhea (missing more than 3 periods in a row)

* May or may not binge or purge

To be diagnosed with bulimia nervosa, the following must be present in our teen:

* Binge eats - eating more food all at once and more than most would eat in one sitting

* Feel a lack of control during binge eating

* Purge the food by making themselves vomit

* Exercise for more than one hour in a row

* Abusing diuretics, diet pills, laxatives or enemas

* Fasting

* Binge and purge regularly over a period of time

* Have a self-image based on their body weight instead of other characteristics

Binge eating in bulimics may include the following:

* Eats more food than most would eat in one sitting

* Feels a lack of control during binge eating

* Overeats to the point of discomfort

* Eats a lot even when not hungry

* Eats alone out of shame

* Feels disgusted with themselves, depressed or very guilty after over eating

* Is concerned about their binge eating

Statistics show that up to 24 million people of all ages and genders suffer from an eating disorder. Anorexia is the third most common chronic illness among adolescents and 95% of those who have eating disorders are between the ages of 12 and 25. Although anorexia is commonly thought to only affect females, "one out of every four pre-teens diagnosed with anorexia is a boy" (Boyse).

> *Statistics show that up to 24 million people of all ages and genders suffer from an eating disorder.*

Contrary to popular belief, eating disorders have little to do with food and much to do with emotional or stress-related issues. At their core, eating disorders involve distorted, self-critical attitudes about weight, food, and body image. Negative thoughts and feelings fuel damaging behaviors as a result.

So why do teens who are in pain choose eating disorders? They do so for control. Research shows those with eating disorders tend to be perfectionists and very hard on themselves (Brownell). The restriction of food is often used to feel control while overeating is used to temporarily relieve negative emotions. Purging is used to overcome feelings of helplessness and self-loathing.

How does a "normal, well-spoken, straight A" teen have an eating disorder? Over time, teens with a tendency toward eating disorders lose perspective on reality and believe the lies inside their minds as well as those that culture reinforces. "If you were skinnier, you would be more lovable," and "You're fat and food is your enemy" are only two examples of the many lies our teens may hear when struggling with either of these disorders. They long to attain the "perfect" image reinforced by the culture, so teens begin practicing routines they believe will help reach their goal of perfection.

Our teens are not the only ones affected by the media's lies when it comes to perfection and body image. Several stars have also been impacted with the "pressure of perfection." Kate Winslett of the blockbuster movie "Titanic" was shocked to view herself after two inches of her thighs were removed so she would look thinner on the front cover of a popular magazine. Her response when she saw the cover? "I am not that thin, and I don't WANT to be that thin!" We must never allow the media to dictate what "beautiful" or "healthy" looks like for our teens.

In order to identify an eating disorder, we must recognize significant warning signs which include:

* Decreased appetite
* Eating a meal and then disappearing into the bathroom
* Depression
* Significant weight loss or weight gain

* An obsession with calorie counting
* Use of laxatives, diet pills or water pills
* Hiding empty containers of food
* Missing or having irregular periods in girls
* Creating "food rituals"
* A distorted self-perception
* An obsession with exercise
* Avoiding eating around others
* Skipping meals or eating small portions
* Cuts and scrapes across tops of finger joints from making themselves vomit
* Cavities or discoloration of teeth from frequent vomiting
* Sleeping problems
* Feeling cold all the time
* Irritability

We must also be aware of the lies that accompany an eating disorder, such as the following:

* You're unlovable.
* You're a fat pig – who would want to look at you?
* You can't eat that – once you start you won't be able to stop.

* If you eat that, you're just like everyone else – weak.

* You have to keep exercising – I don't care how much it hurts.

* Don't listen to them. They just want you to be fat like them.

* You will be fat if you don't throw up – and since you ate, you can't eat tomorrow.

As you can see, the lies that invade the minds of those struggling with eating disorders are ruthless. We must combat these lies by reminding our teen we love them, and most importantly, that God loves them. When we judge, we only push them further into their disease - and it is a disease.

EDNOS is the most commonly diagnosed eating disorder in clinical settings. EDNOS stands for "Eating Disorders Not Otherwise Specified" ("Eating Disorders"). Those who do not struggle with the specific signs associated with anorexia or bulimia can still suffer from an eating disorder. EDNOS have specific criteria that must be recognized, including the following:

* One who meets the criteria for anorexia, but still has a menstrual cycle

* One who meets all the diagnostic criteria for anorexia but is still within the normal weight range despite significant weight loss

* One who chews, but spits out/does not swallow food

* One who meets all the criteria for bulimia but their binging/purging is less than twice a week for a duration of less than three months

* One who severely restricts food, counts calories, and purges after eating

Those with EDNOS often look healthy, yet their mortality rate is higher than both anorexics and bulimics. If you see any of these signs in your teen, be sure to have your physician examine them right away.

If your teen is struggling with unhealthy choices in the area of eating, there are some practical things you can do to help. Following is a list of proven suggestions:

➢ Insist that your teen get professional help and let them know that this is non-negotiable. Accompany them on appointments and remind them that you are there to support them. Remember, teens with eating disorders do not believe they need help, so we must help them take steps toward health. If our child had pneumonia, we would get them to a doctor. Treating eating disorders with professional help is crucial.

➢ Tell your teen you are worried. Be specific and non-judgmental as you share your concerns.

➢ Don't talk about your teen's appearance, even if you are giving a compliment. This will only isolate them more and make them feel more alone. Focus instead on their thoughtful actions, or something they have accomplished at school.

➢ Let your teen know that you are there to listen if they need to talk. Stay positive and encouraging.

➢ Talk with someone about your concerns. Counselors, teachers, and other parents of teens with eating disorders can be a great source of support.

➢ Serve as a good role model by eating healthy meals and demonstrate a balanced exercise routine.

➢ Learn as much as possible about eating disorders. When you Google the words "eating disorders" in your internet browser, you will find a great deal of information as well as parenting tips. *"Hope, Help, and Healing for Eating Disorders"* by Gregory L. Jantz is also a great book for treating the whole person when an eating disorder is present.

➢ Pray for your teen and ask God to give you the ability to interact with them in a positive, loving, and supportive role.

Understand that your teen may become defensive when first confronted. They have adopted the eating disorder as a coping skill, and they may be very reluctant to let go of it. If your teen becomes secretive, it is due to their illness, not their relationship with you. Continue to provide the care they need, regardless of their reluctance. Remember, you are battling a disease, not your child.

Meal times are also a very delicate part of the disease. If your teen is in treatment, ask your treatment team how to appropriately plan mealtimes. Invite your teen to grocery shop with you so that purchasing food is done in agreement. Avoid talking about calories or fat content during meals. Strive to keep the conversation light-hearted throughout the meal. Providing a positive environment is important.

If your teen decides they want to help you prepare the meal as a means of control, simply suggest your teen set the table, or get their hands washed. Once the meal is complete, planning a game or another activity as a family is a positive way of providing alternatives to purging or over-exercising.

Parenting a child with an eating disorder can be frustrating and exhausting, and it is most important to understand what to do in order to correct the problem. The mom I mentioned at the beginning of this chapter found success.

When Ashley returned home from the hospital, her family followed strict doctor's orders. Although Ashley refused to eat and there were many tears at times, her family stood strong. They gently reminded her that if doctor's orders could not be followed at home, they would be forced to place Ashley back in the hospital and they would follow through with doing so because they loved her. They continually reminded Ashley of God's love as well as theirs, and over time, they saw Ashley return, physically and mentally.

"I finally have my daughter back," Ashley's mom told me months later.

As previously mentioned, the media plays a part in many of our teen's decisions to adopt an eating disorder. Videos, chat rooms, discussion boards and websites are often dangerous places for promoting destructive behaviors. Be aware if your child spends a great amount of time on the internet. Websites which promote eating disorders include the words "pro-ana" for anorexia, and "pro-mia" for bulimia. Know what to look for when reviewing your child's internet history.

Remember, if you are concerned your child may have an eating disorder, follow up with your doctor immediately. Share your concerns and allow your doctor to take your teen's weight, height and body mass index. The more information your doctor has, the better, so the appropriate direction can be given.

If you are unable to reach your doctor and you suspect an eating disorder may be present in your teen's life, Contact the National Eating Disorders Association at 1-800-931-2237. They will be able to give you more information and guide you in the direction of those who can assist you.

Remember, God is in the restoration business and He is able to bring healing both emotionally and physically to your child. He will replace the lies with His truth and set them free to celebrate the beautiful person they are in Christ.

PARENT PAUSE:

1. How will you talk with your teen about the warning signs of an eating disorder?

2. How can you help support your teen or their friends if an eating disorder is diagnosed?

3. If treatment is needed, who will be your source of support?

CHAPTER FOUR

NOTHING GOOD HAPPENS AFTER MIDNIGHT

"Love is an act of endless forgiveness."

-Jean Vanier

I couldn't wait to date. As a young teen, I dreamed that my date would pick me up at the door with roses, extend his hand and blissfully walk me to the car as he stared adoringly into my eyes. I never gave much thought to what age I would be until one evening my Dad sent me into shock. When I asked how old I had to be to date, he responded with a smirk, "Forty." While that seems funny now, as a young teen, my world stopped. "Forty? Forty?? I will be nearly DEAD by then!" Little did I know how young forty would eventually feel.

Fortunately, Dad's sense of humor increased and the age I could date decreased. I began dating when I was sixteen, but the rules my parents enforced were strict. My curfew was midnight – period. It didn't matter where I was going, whose parents let them stay out late or how much I begged. I knew the boundary, and I knew better than to ask for extended time. While there were a few special occasions when I was allowed additional time, they were VERY rare.

Dad had a philosophy and it determined my curfew. His mantra was, "Nothing good happens after midnight." Research shows that my dad got it right. The Insurance Institute for Highway Safety reports that 16% of all teenage motor vehicle deaths in 2011 occurred between midnight and 3 a.m., one of the highest percentages of the day. ("Fatality Facts 2011")

I'm sure my parents knew statistics, but they always led me to believe that my curfew was midnight because that's the latest they could stay awake. I never returned from a date that one of them wasn't waiting in the living room to be sure I was home safely. If I was sitting in the driveway and the clock struck midnight, I got the ol' flicker of the porch light. That was a sign for me to come in – NOW.

While the dating years are usually an exciting time for teens, they can be challenging for parents. Open communication is key when it comes to talking with our teens about dating, and knowing some important facts can help aid the conversation.

It's best to talk about dating with your child in the "tween" years. If you wait until after 13, you have probably waited too late. By age twelve, our "tweens" have been exposed to television, video games and online media which attempt to give our teens guidelines for dating. When talking with your "tween," remember to keep the communication open, alive and upbeat. When we begin to lecture or scold, they tune us out.

To begin, we should identify dating as the opportunity for a boy and a girl to spend time getting to know one another in a variety of settings. Exclusive dating is when a boy and girl date one another and it is steady and serious. Inclusive dating refers to kids spending time with several friends of the opposite sex. An inclusive date can be three girls and two guys who meet at someone's house for pizza and a movie. Many parents, including this one, encourage inclusive dating prior to exclusive dating. Inclusive dating provides teens with a great opportunity to hone their opposite-sex-relationship skills in a safe and accountable environment.

Dating is not a skill teens acquire in the classroom, so as parents, we must give them general guidelines. Teach them the importance of mutual respect. Philippians 2:3-5 (NLT) says, "Don't be selfish; don't try to impress others. Be humble, thinking of others as better than yourselves. Don't look out only for your own interests, but take an interest in others, too. You must have the same attitude that Christ Jesus had." Remind your teen that they are to treat the one they date with respect, and vice-versa. If respect is not demonstrated on both sides, the relationship is not a healthy one. If your teen is unclear on what healthy respect looks like, ask questions about various scenarios and how they would view a situation. For example,

"If your date calls you names that are hurtful and then says it's a joke, do you consider that behavior disrespectful?" By asking such questions, you will get an idea of how your teen views him/herself and others, as well as their knowledge of healthy boundaries in relationships.

It is also necessary to ask your teen questions to have a full and complete understanding of who they are dating. Questions such as: "How did you meet? Where does he/she go to school? Where does he/she live and who do they live with?" are helpful when uncovering information. If there are mutual friends, make some calls and politely inquire about the person your teen is dating. No one said you can't do a little "detective work" along the way...just do it with wisdom.

Your teen must also feel free to be themselves on a date. Compromising standards is what often causes failure in dating relationships. As teens stay true to who they were created to be, dating will be fun. In a recent survey, statistics showed that teens would much rather establish a long term relationship with someone who is fun than with someone considered "hot" (TeenGirlNow.com). While looks are often the initial attraction, they quickly fade when "ugly" emerges from the inside. Integrity and character are valuable.

When Tommy came to visit my office, he was very upset about his girlfriend breaking up with him. They went to church together, and he could not understand how she could dump him. He was the quarterback of the football team, voted "best looking" at school and was always the life of the party. As Tommy shared more of his story, it became clear why his girlfriend left him. Tommy believed he was entitled to call his girlfriend a "broad." This was embarrassing to Tommy's girlfriend and she asked him to stop. The term always got him a laugh from his peers, so he refused, telling her she was unreasonable. Tommy found that his good looks and charm were not enough to excuse his hurtful behavior and he lost his girlfriend as a result. As Tommy and I discussed his options, he agreed that an apology was in order and agreed to make better choices.

What emanates from the heart is what we believe about God, ourselves and others.

How do we help develop character in our teens and help them make good choices? We focus on the heart. What emanates from the heart is what we believe about God, ourselves and others. Teens find other teens attractive who feel good about themselves and we feel best about ourselves when we're living true to our heart's convictions. When teens are living by Godly morals and standards that have been taught in the home, they make better choices for their dating lives.

God gives some great guidelines in His Word about dating and, as parents, we must reinforce these guidelines in order to offer our teens wisdom on dating.

II Corinthians 6:14 says, "Do not be yoked together with unbelievers. For what do righteousness and wickedness have in common? Or what fellowship can light have with darkness?" God is reminding us of a very important command that will save our teens much heartache in the long run. If your teen is a Christian, they are to date and marry only those who have a heart after God's heart. Statistics show that when teens date non-Christians they are more likely to marry non-Christians. When our Christian teen enters into a relationship with a non-Christian, inevitable heartache is the result because it goes against God's Word. Your teen can avoid the drama that often goes with dating by simply dating God's way.

When teens take their boyfriend or girlfriend to church in hopes they will FIND Jesus, we call this "missionary dating." Taking another to church is a great thing to do when teens are friends, but dating him/her after they have FOUND Jesus is what the Bible commands. Our teens are commanded to only date those who serve Jesus Christ. Notice I use the word serve. We know many teens claim to be Christians, but we will "know them by their fruit." If your teen is dating someone who is claiming to know Christ but living like the devil when they are with your teen, it is not a healthy relationship. Gently talk with your teen and remind them they deserve God's best.

Several issues arise when our teens begin dating and parents often ask for advice. The following are some questions I have heard most often.

First, at what age should a teen begin dating? While many factors must be taken into consideration, and each situation is different, accountability must be part of your decision. Is your teen accountable for their dating life? Do they talk with you? Do they have a Christian mentor or other adult in their life with whom they will share their dating details? If not, accountability must be put into place before dating begins. When your teen is ready to have someone remind them of Godly standards for their relationship, they may be ready to date. Having an adult who will talk with them about their temptations, and one who will pray with them about their relationship is a sign that your teen is ready to stand accountable for their dating life.

If you would like to be your teen's accountability partner, be sure that you are able to listen objectively. Some things may be tough to hear and you must be able to listen without criticism or judgment. This can be extremely difficult because we want the best for our children and they are a reflection of us.

If you are unable to be your child's accountability partner, allow youth directors, grandparents, pastors, teachers or other Godly adults you trust to speak into your child's life. It's amazing how our teens often "hear" the truth we have been telling them for years when it is spoken from another adult's lips. Pray for those who are speaking into your child's life, and pray for your teen as they listen.

Another question we must take into consideration is, "Are they dating for the right reasons?" Many of our teens begin dating for fun and friendship. Others date because they are lacking a true sense of identity. Reminding our teens that they are complete with or without a date is important. Two halves don't make a whole; two WHOLE people make a WHOLE relationship. Remind your teen of their special qualities, and reinforce the importance of finding someone to date who appreciates those positive qualities. Talk with them about the "fantasy" aspect of teen dating. Too many times teens grow disappointed because their date does not live up to the fantasy planted in their mind by the media. Discuss reasonable and fair expectations of dating with your teen.

Another great thing to do is have your teen list the qualities they are looking for in a future mate. Not only will this initiate interesting discussion, it gives your teen something concrete to remember when making their choices. Teach your teen how to recognize others with positive qualities as well as how to identify those who may present themselves in one way, but live another. Anyone can say they are a Christian, but if your teen's date is mean, controlling, cussing, yelling, checking phones, making fun of how your teen looks or giving the cold shoulder when they don't get their way, help your teen understand the detriment to their relationship. Remind your teen that they should want to date someone who will help them become the best they can be. More than likely, they did NOT include negative characteristics on their list of qualifications for a future mate.

If you are the parent of a teen who refuses to conduct their dating life God's way, you will witness heartache. There is no way around it. Why? Because "God is love" (1 John 4:16) and when there is no God in the relationship, there is no "real" love, only feelings of love. There is a positive side, however. Pain is often a great motivator, so take the opportunity during your teen's heartbreak to share the truth of love with them. Give an "account for the hope that is in you" (I Peter 3:15) and share how much God loves them. Remind your teen He has a powerful plan for their life when they surrender to Him. While you are not promising life will be perfect, you are promising someone who will help them in making the right decisions.

Another frequently asked question is, "What if I don't like the person my teen is dating?" If you are like most parents, there is the likelihood that at least one will come along that you don't hold in high regard. Most of us can probably look back and remember at least one date that our parents were less than thrilled about. If there is no physical, emotional, spiritual or psychological danger to your teen and you just don't like their date, stand by and try to gently lead. Telling them you don't care for the person often drives them further away. Talk with your child about why they enjoy dating that individual. Keeping an open line of communication will help you know more of how your child is being affected in the relationship. Downgrading, fault-finding or belittling their date will only shut them off from you.

If you find that your teen is trying to "save" the person that you are not fond of, discuss the hopes your teen has and list their limits. Listing their limits in the relationship will help your teen realize how little control they have over the person they are dating. I will warn you, however, that it may take longer than you hope for your teen to realize they cannot change their date. This can be hard to watch as a parent, but stand by because they will need you soon enough.

If you have set age limits for your teen, make sure you abide by them. If your teen is sixteen and you do not permit him/her to date anyone over the age of eighteen, the answer is simply, "No." There are many things that we can control as parents, but one we have no control over is the heart. We do, however, have control over WHEN and at what age our teen can spend time with the opposite sex.

I know a mom whose daughter insisted on seeing her older "crush." She would sneak out, talk with the older boy without her parent's consent and invite him over to a friend's house where she would stay. Frustrated, the mom decided to try a different approach. The mom told her daughter she could spend time with the older boy under one condition – she must be present everywhere they went. The daughter reluctantly consented, and the mom accompanied her at all times. Although it was somewhat taxing on the mom, it paid off. The older boy got tired of mom tagging along and decided to end the relationship. Although the daughter was upset, she realized the older boy was not willing to make the sacrifice in order to spend time with her and the relationship dissolved.

If you sense your child's dating situation is dangerous and you have legitimate concerns, discuss them with your teen. Remember, the way you present things has a lot to do with how your concerns will be received. Be sure to focus on the behavior, and not the person. For example, you might say, "It really concerns me that I hear your date yelling at you on the phone. Do they treat everyone around them that way?"

Parents, based on statistics, we have reason to be on guard about our teen's safety in the area of dating. One in three teenagers report being hit, punched, kicked, slapped, choked or physically hurt by their date. One in four teenage girls who have been in relationships reveal they have been pressured to perform oral sex or engage in intercourse. More than one in four teenage girls in a relationship report enduring repeated verbal abuse, and only 33% who have been in, or known about, an abusive relationship said they have told anyone about it ("Dating Abuse Statistics").

Furthermore, less than 25% of teens say they have discussed dating violence with their parents (T.E.A.R). All of these statistics give us great reason to continually be involved in our teen's dating life. If you find that your teen is dating someone abusive or who is an addict, get professional help. These are areas that can force your teen onto a road they are not intended to travel. Seek help immediately if you are made aware of any such happenings in your teen's relationship.

When your teen is with their date in your home, insist that they stay in rooms where others are present or where they may be easily accessed. All doors should remain open. Talking with the parents of your teen's date can also be helpful. Let them know that you have expectations in your home and find out those of their home as well. This may help you in making decisions about where your teen spends most of their time.

Be sure to plan things that keep your teen and their date close to you at times so you can observe their behavior. Invite them to play a game with your family or spend time watching movies. This may give you a more positive perspective of your teen's date, or give you more cause for concerns that need to be addressed. Planning group events at your home gives you an opportunity to observe how your teen and their date speak to one another and interact with others of the same and opposite sex. As a matter of fact, more and more parents are encouraging their teens to "group date."

Group dating is a great way to help our teens grow socially as well as learn about the opposite sex. Group dating can also be fun and gives our teen an opportunity to experience "built-in" accountability. When teens are with a group, statistics show that they are much less likely to be tempted in the area of sex (discussed in Chapter 5) because others are present. Teens often realize that having friends of the opposite sex is wonderful, and to transform the friendship into a dating relationship can drastically change the friendship. As a result, teens place more thought into developing "dating" relationships.

Teens also become aware of the different personalities in the opposite sex when "group dating." Hanging out with youth groups or close friends from school or church is a great way for teens to befriend those with similar moral and spiritual values while making decisions about "dating." Invite the group to your home and get to know the parents of those within the group. More than likely, your teen will date someone with similar interests, so find out all you can about those that your teen enjoys being around.

Some practical exercises that we can use to teach our kids to date God's way are below:

➤ Recommend that your teen and their date pray together. It may sound awkward at first, but just "talking" to God before or during a date is a powerful way to keep the relationship focused in the right direction.

➤ Teach your teen that being a good listener can make for a great date. There's no need to solve their date's problems, but listening is a huge part of showing respect in a relationship.

➢ Suggest your teen do a devotional with their date. This is a great way for your teen to find out if there are "deal breakers" in the relationship. For example, if your teen is dating someone of a different religion, recognizing that there are things they cannot agree on might ultimately be the end of the relationship. It's better to find out on a date than after they are married.

➢ Give your teen some ideas for great dates that don't compromise their convictions. A museum, local zoo, going for coffee or ice cream, a carnival, a fair or a Christian concert are great alternatives for a fun dating experience.

A friend of mine shared her families' guidelines for dating and I have permission to share them with you. They have worked well for the teenagers in her family, and they are as follows:

➢ Girls, your date must meet you at the door and must greet us as parents before you leave.

➢ Boys, you must meet your date at the door when you pick her up. You must also meet/greet her parents before leaving for your date.

➢ All dates must be to a public place.

➢ You may only ride with those who have been driving longer than six months, and those who have not been drinking or using drugs of any kind.

➢ If you are going to be late for curfew for any reason, you must call. If there is no answer, you must leave a message.

➤ Always have and execute a plan if you find yourself in a compromising/uncomfortable position and let your parents know what your plan will be before you begin dating.

➤ Avoid situations that bring temptation for sexual contact.

➤ You must always inform your parents of your plans, as well as when plans change. Again, if no answer, leave a message.

➤ Modest dress is a must for all dates. (Discuss what that looks like before your daughter/son begins dating).

➤ You may only date someone within two years of your own age (remembering each child is different, this is a wise suggestion for many reasons).

➤ No more than two dates per week.

➤ No use of alcohol, drugs or tobacco.

➤ No dating a friend's boyfriend or ex-boyfriend/girlfriend or ex-girlfriend.

Another friend of mine adds, "No first dates at a movie theatre...it is just too dark and too tempting."

If you are a single parent, please remember that you have an opportunity to model what "healthy dating" looks like. The standards you hold for your teen should be the same you hold for yourself. If you find there is a difficult situation you need to address and your teen is the opposite sex, be sure to search out a youth director or Godly friend of the opposite sex who can help.

Parents, the most important thing to remember is to try to relax and help your teen enjoy these years. If your teen expresses no desire to date, don't be alarmed. Some teens focus on careers, school work, scholarships and friendships before beginning their dating journey.

Remember, you have great opportunity to speak into the life of your teen regarding their dating life and when you guide them God's way, great things can transpire.

PARENT PAUSE:

1. What will you do to help guide your teen in making the right choices for their dating life?

2. How will a list of dating guidelines be implemented in your home? What will you include in those guidelines?

3. What have you found are the greatest challenges as your teen begins to date? How will you approach those challenges?

CHAPTER FIVE

PURITY
AND
GOD'S PROMISES

"Chastity is the most unpopular of the Christian virtues."

-C.S. Lewis

Statistics show that over half of all teens have had sexual relations before they graduate from high school ("Teens and Sex"). If you're like me, my heart breaks when I read such statistics. After all, most of our kids had absolutely no interest in the opposite sex until their teenage years. Overnight, they wake up with raging hormones and their whole world changes. Unfortunately, our teens have been desensitized by the bombardment of sexual images on television, the internet, movies, advertisements and more. What can we do as parents to protect our teens? We must take a more active role in teaching teens God's standards and design for sex.

Many times, we are afraid of saying the wrong thing, so we ignore the topic, hoping they will learn it somehow. They will, but chances are great that they will not learn it in a healthy way. If we want our teens to value the act of sex in marriage, we must pass on values of sexual purity. While reminding our teens that sexual feelings are normal, we must also suggest that they are not physically, emotionally or spiritually ready to act on such feelings. Our teens must understand that sex is more than a physical act. It is laden with emotion and potential consequences that they are in no way prepared to face. Unplanned pregnancies and disease are often the results of premature sexual encounters, and spiritual and emotional ties bring great heartbreak when sex occurs outside the confines of marriage.

As I visit with teens about sex during counseling sessions in my conferences, I often use the analogy of a hunter. The reason men like to hunt is the thrill of the hunt, but what happens when the man catches the hunt? You know the answer – he kills it! Once the catch is made, the excitement is over. Allow me to break it down into plain terms. Once a young lady and young man engage in sexual acts that should only be entertained during marriage, the excitement soon fades and hearts are broken.

The Bible is very clear about sex outside of marriage. I Corinthians 7:2-3 says, "There is so much immorality, each man should have his own wife, and each woman her own husband. The husband should fulfill his marital duty to his wife, and likewise the wife to her husband." Our teens must realize that there is only one "first time" when engaging in sexual behavior. When teens are sexually active before marriage, their future spouse gets left-overs and vice versa. Philippians 4:8 says, "...whatever is true, whatever is noble, whatever is right, whatever is pure, whatever is lovely, whatever is admirable – if anything is excellent or praiseworthy – think about such things." David reminds us that a young person can stay pure by obeying God's Word and following its rules in Psalm 119:9. Purity, by definition, is anything free from contamination or pollution. Teens lose purity in their relationships when they act like they are married and they are not.

The act of sex outside the boundaries of marriage produces severe consequences. The fact that nearly one-third of all girls in the United States will get pregnant in their teenage years is a sobering thought. According to Pregnant Teen Help, the United States has the highest teenage pregnancy rate and teen births in the western-industrialized world. ("Teen Pregnancy Rates") The following statistics will surely help encourage us to talk with our teen about sex:

- Every year, approximately 750,000 teenagers will get pregnant.

- Unmarried teenagers having children account for 24% of all unmarried expectant mothers.

- More than 2/3 of all teenagers who have a baby will not graduate from high school.

It is also imperative to note that eighteen percent of the females in the United States who obtain abortions are teenagers ("National Reproductive Health").

As these statistics drive us to talk with our teens, we must discriminate between the age of our teen and what amount of information we need to share. I have worked with too many parents who believed their teen had not been exposed to sexual content, only to find their child pregnant or sexually-active. Girls at age ten are having children, and although we attempt to protect our tweens and teens, kids share information about sex out of curiosity. It is best that the truths about sex come from you before the mainstream media or friends have the opportunity to teach it for you. Living in denial that our "tween" or "teen" has not been exposed to sexual information can be damaging and many unwanted results may occur.

Parental resources are available to help aid in talking with your teen about sex from a Godly perspective. Focus on the Family offers these suggestions when talking with your teen about sex and puberty:

➢ Give your child facts about reproduction. Explaining sex as an act of love and one that produces new life can help maintain innocence.

➢ Examine your own beliefs about sex. If you are hesitant to share the facts about sex, do you have a mindset that sex is something other than what it was designed by God to be?

➤ Share the details of sex over a period of years, not all in one sitting. This is not a one-time conversation.

➤ Give information on a "need to know" basis. If your five-year-old wants to know how the baby got inside your tummy, it is not necessary to give all the details.

➤ If your teen asks questions and you don't know the answer, be honest. Teens will have much more respect for parents who research the facts rather than make something up ("Talking About Sex and Puberty").

Reminding our teens that pick-up lines are used to CROSS lines is essential.

The feeling of being "in love" may occur many times before our teen gets married. Consequently, temptation may come as a result of such feelings. Teach your teen some common phrases that may be used in an attempt to manipulate them into sexual behavior. Phrases or pick-up lines like these are warning signs:

- "Oh baby, you know I love you, I just want to be close to you."

- "I will love you forever. Don't worry, I'm not going anywhere."

- "You're the only one I have ever felt this way about."

- "If you really loved me, you would _____."

Too many times I have counseled teenage girls who believed the last line. They wanted desperately to be loved, and were swept up in the moment when asked to prove their love. Reminding our teens that pick-up lines are used to CROSS lines is essential.

Girls are not the only ones being pressured to compromise their purity. The Urban Institute's National Survey of Adolescent Males conducted a study of the sexual activities of teen boys and found startling statistics. Among 16 year olds, forty-seven percent have engaged in vaginal intercourse while fifty-three percent of 15-19 year olds have been masturbated by a female. Forty-nine percent of these same boys claim they have received oral sex. One in 10 teen males had engaged in anal intercourse. ("Reducing Teen STD Risk")

Unfortunately, statistics do not vary greatly between Christians and non-Christians. According to Answering Christianity, one in four Christian teen girls has a sexually transmitted disease (STD); therefore, males and females are at high risk for contracting an STD when sexually active. ("Latest Study") The Centers for Disease Control reports that about 20 million new STD infections occur every year. ("CDC Fact Sheet") Even more alarming, nearly 50 percent of these new cases occur in young people between the ages of 15 and 24. Half of all new HIV infections occur in teenagers ("Teens and Young Adults").

There is a TRIED and TRUE method to prevent the spread of STDs, and that is ABSTINENCE. I challenge any organization which states that there are other "full-proof" methods. Excuse me for getting on my soap box for a moment, but if you aren't having sexual interaction with another person, it's IMPOSSI-BLE to contract an STD! This includes oral sex. STDs are just as easily contracted through oral sex as through vaginal or anal sex. We MUST teach our teens about the physical dangers sex brings and that oral sex IS a part of having sex. "Lipstick Parties" or "Rainbow Parties" spread STDs through oral sex. These parties involve females wearing various shades of lipstick who take turns giving males oral sex in sequence. As a result, the male's penis is left with a "rainbow" around it. Some argue that "rainbow parties" are an urban legend, while others argue they are real. Regardless, we know that the amount of teenagers reportedly having oral sex is astronomical. We must teach and remind our teens that God views oral sex as part of the "sexual act" and His heart is broken when any act of sex is performed outside the boundaries of marriage. As with any other sin, there are consequences. While He loves us, He does hold us accountable when we go against His command to abstain from any "hint" of sexual immorality or acts until marriage (Ephesians 5:3).

Sexting is another way teens are sharing themselves without engaging in the physical act of sex. Teens participate in "sexting" by sending sexually-explicit images or text messages. Various smart phone applications (apps) allow images to be shared with known and unknown viewers. (The names of these apps are available in Chapter 7). Those who engage in "sexting" do so to gain interest from the recipient, but the interest is usually short-lived, and great damage is often done as a result. Many teens find themselves as the negative focus when a picture or message is shared. Teens often forget that once their image or message is in cyber-space, it is available for anyone to retrieve. A picture can be circulated throughout school within minutes when teens share images on their phones. The result may be extreme ridicule, rejection and lowered self-esteem for the "sender" of the image or message. Our teens must remember that if they would not be comfortable sharing their picture or message in the local newspaper, with their pastor or with their parent, it is best they don't send it.

According to the Christian Post, Christian teens are far from exempt when it comes to "sexting." The Post claims 22 percent of girls sent or posted explicit images of themselves

According to the Christian Post, Christian teens are far from exempt when it comes to "sexting."

while 18 percent of boys did the same. (Sun) Your teen should know that sexting is also illegal now in many states and the penalties can be severe for both the sender AND receiver of such messages. Legal-

Match.com defines sexting as "the act of transmitting sexually explicit messages, primarily through the use of cell phone text messaging. The messages usually contain illicit photographs or video links depicting the person sending them. They can be sent from one person to another, and sometimes they may be sent to mass recipients." (LaMance) Most states include language requiring that the photo be of a minor or a child.

Legal penalties for sexting may include:

- Fines not exceeding $1,000
- Mandatory counseling (especially for minors)
- Possible jail time
- Restriction of driving privileges for minors

Also, depending on the circumstances, sexting can either result in a misdemeanor or more serious felony charges. In most cases, felony charges will result if the sexting involves child pornography and the recipient is not a minor. Felony charges usually involve very high criminal fines and prison sentences of greater than one year.

How do we lead our teen in the right direction while surrounded with a culture that is saturated with sex? We must teach them the TRUTH. When we teach the truth of God's Word and age appropriate facts about sex, our teens are better prepared to make the right choices when temptation comes. Remember, NO teen is exempt from temptation.

Other helpful facts for talking with your teen about sex come from Barbara and Dennis Rainey of Family Life. The following are crucial:

1. Remind your teen that sex is for procreation in marriage.

2. Sex is for pleasure in marriage. Proverbs 5:19 says, "As a loving hind and a graceful doe, let her breasts satisfy you at all times; be exhilarated always with her love." That is not Playboy 5:19; that's Proverbs 5:19. The Song of Solomon is another book of the Bible that offers insight into the pleasures of sex within marriage.

3. Model a warm, affectionate, honest marriage in front of your children.

4. Sex was created to be enjoyed by ONLY a man and a woman in marriage. Our teens must be reminded that just because some groups validate homosexual behavior, it is not right in God's eyes. Our teens must learn to hate the sin (see Romans 1:26-27) while loving the sinner.

5. Sex outside of marriage is a sin. Use the following points to develop a clear, well-thought-out explanation on how God uses sexual purity for our good:

   a. You have no guilt, no shame, and no emotional scars when you hold to a standard of sexual holiness. You don't hear any accusing voices in your own conscience.

   b. You won't be tempted to compare your future spouse with a past lover.

   c. You have ZERO risk of a sexually transmitted disease.

    d.   You will not face the possibility of bearing a child out of wedlock.

    e.   You will have much-needed training in self-control and self-denial. (Rainey)

Many parents ask about the importance of teaching "safe sex." Focus on the Family says it well. "There is no sex that is 'safe' outside of marriage." ("Sex Education") While pregnancy may OR MAY NOT be avoided, the emotional and spiritual scars that occur are anything but "safe."

What if our teen has already had sex? The most important thing is to react as calmly as possible. While difficult, we must keep the lines of communication open if we want to help our teen. They will only hide their failures further if we shame them. Remember, "For all have sinned and fall short of the glory of God" (Romans 3:23). While heartbreaking, it is possible for our teen to begin again.

To help your teen after sexual immorality has occurred, let them know that there is nothing they can do to lose your love. While you are disappointed, ask your teen to tell you how you can support them to make better choices in the future. Then, listen as they talk with you. Most likely, your teen will tell you what they need. Do they need help with setting boundaries? If so, help them by setting boundaries for future dating situations (see Chapter 4). If your teen was sexually active while spending the night at a friend's house, suggest that future sleepovers be hosted at your home.

You must also let your teen know that you forgive them and that they must allow God's forgiveness to purify them. Then, pray with your teen. Ask God to help guard their heart and to help them become stronger in this area of temptation.

Some other suggestions are as follows:

➢ Take your teen to a trusted physician to check for STDs and pregnancy.

➢ Set firm family rules. Let them know that you will be deeply involved in helping them avoid temptation in the future by setting stricter limits on the amount of time they are allowed to spend with members of the opposite sex. This might mean that he or she won't be allowed to use the car without you or another adult along for the ride.

➢ Find an accountability or abstinence group for your teen to participate in. Ask your pastor for guidance and schedule counseling with a Christian counselor or youth leader.

➢ Keep your teen busy with supervised activities. "Busy" and "supervised" is a winning combination and keeps accountability at a higher rate.

If you suspect your teen may be having sex but are uncertain, watch for the following signs:

• Condoms and personal lubricants are present: These are often secured in wallets, at the back of dresser drawers or at the bottom of trashcans. A used condom will look like the finger of a rubber glove and will be sticky to the touch.

- Washing their clothes and frequent bathing: Teens often wash clothes in order to hide the smell of semen.

- Sudden interest in your whereabouts or trips you're planning away from home: If your teen is mysteriously in the house during unexpected hours of the day or beds that were made in the morning strangely appear unmade in the afternoon, be aware (Sorvese).

- Inflated self-image: Promiscuous children believe that sex makes them more mature.

- Breaking curfew: Teens must be accountable for all time spent away from home.

- Health issues: Recurring bladder infections, enlarged testes, penile chaffing, pain in the lower abdomen and yeast infections are all signs that a child is not only engaging in sex, but that he or she may have contracted an STD.

- Sleepovers with friends who have siblings: Sometimes teens pretend to be best friends with one person while secretly "hooking up" with the brother or sister. Sleepovers give ample opportunity for sexual encounters in the middle of the night. Remember, not every parent is as vigilant or Christian as you would hope them to be.

- Gang membership: Although rare, girls who join gangs will allow themselves to be gang raped as part of their horrific initiation process. Be vigilant if your girl suddenly opts for dark urban clothing styles and insists on wearing certain colors while avoiding others.

- Alcohol, cigarette and drug usage: There is a sad overlap between illegal substance abuse and teenage sexuality. This indicates you have a broader dilemma on your hands.

According to Crosswalk.com, statistics show that fifty-five percent of Christian male teens and seventy percent of female teens who have had sex now say they wish they had not. (Ferrel) The TRUTH about sex will protect our teen from regret, heartache and consequences that may be life-altering.

Most importantly, remind your teen that self-respect is a key to avoiding sexual infractions. When we respect ourselves, we are less likely to engage in behavior that is damaging. Remind your teen that they are worthy of God's best, and that they will be grateful for waiting on God's best. After all, God created sex for our enjoyment and He will bless it when it is within the confines of marriage.

As you approach your teen about the sensitive subject of sex, be sure to do so in love. Remember, "Love never fails" (I Corinthians 13:8).

PARENT PAUSE:

1. What have you found is the greatest challenge in talking with your teen about sex?

2. What is your plan if you find your teen is sexually active before marriage?

3. In what ways have you successfully protected your teen from the sexually explicit information offered by this culture?

CHAPTER SIX

BFF

"The best mirror is an old friend."

-*George Herbert*

Growing up, I had five close friends, otherwise known as "The Group." From elementary through high school, we shared everything from happiness to heartbreak, and we were inseparable. I am honored to say that three of them are still some of my closest friends today. Regular lunches and emails keep our 36 year friendship growing strong. It is only because the other two moved out of town that we are not as close.

Friendships are an important part of life at any age. As parents, we long to have those in our lives who we can connect with on an intimate level. The longing for friendship never changes, and great friendships can begin at any stage of life.

In the formative years, we teach our children how to "play well with others." During the pre-teen and teen years, friendships are developed as a result of these skills. As parents, we can have much influence in the way our teens choose friends, but ultimately, it will be their decision. So how do we help guide our teens in developing healthy friendships?

Some teens need the "basics" of friendship and as parents, we can certainly provide them. Following is a list of suggestions that have proven to help build positive friendships among teens:

➢ Be honest. While everything doesn't have to be said, there are some things that must be said. If you see a friend being disrespectful to someone, don't join in. Respectfully call them out.

➢ Be a good listener. No one wants to be friends with someone who only talks about themselves.

➢ Speak kindly. Use language that is edifying, and avoid words that are hurtful or offensive.

➢ Be a giver. Offer to help your friend with a project or to pray for them when they are going through something tough.

➢ Have fun. Friendships should be filled with times of laughter. If strife is what fills most of your friendship, re-evaluate.

➢ Learn to compromise. Give and take is part of friendship.

➢ Be supportive. Be someone's cheerleader. Encourage your friend and let them know you are there for them and that you believe in them.

➢ Maintain your boundaries and respect the boundaries of others. Remember the adage, "If you don't stand for something, you will fall for anything."

Just because a friend is comfortable with something, doesn't mean you must be comfortable with it also.

➤ Be yourself. True friends will like the real you.

Conversations with our teen about friendship choices will be ongoing. This is not a "one time talk." We will have many opportunities to identify positive characteristics in those with whom our children associate. The more positive we are, the more likely they are to listen. If we become "preachy" or demanding, they are much less likely to hear us.

Asking our teen about the qualities they value in friends and how their friendships are beneficial is a great way to dialogue with them. Many times, friendships are one-sided, so reminding our teen that friendships are give AND take will be an important part of the discussions. When talking with our teens, we may find that they are more on the giving end of a friendship than on the receiving end. While giving is good, and scriptural, there comes a time where we must evaluate the motive of the heart when a friendship is one-sided. Discuss lopsided friendships with your teen. Ask them how they feel when they do more giving than receiving.

If you see that the friendship is unbalanced, but your teen does not, try this exercise. Have your teen draw a line down the middle of a piece of paper. On one side of the paper, have your teen write their name at the top of the page. Under their name, have your teen write all of the things they have done to contribute to the friendship. On the other side of the line, have your teen write their friend's name and write down all the things they feel the friend has done to contribute to the friendship. Discuss the results with your teen and have them talk about how it feels to be the more giving person in the relationship. If your teen decides they will continue the friendship, pray for the protection of your teen's heart and that they will quickly see the truth about the friendship. If they complain about the friendship at some point, refer back to the piece of paper and gently remind them of the imbalance the two of you discussed when you did the exercise together. Teens will usually walk away from unbalanced friendships, but it is often hard to stand by and allow them to discover this truth on their own.

We know that there can be great drama in teen friendships. Fortunately, the drama usually subsides as quickly as the circumstances because neither lasts. Our teen may be "best friends" with someone in their class for a semester, but when the class ends, so does the friendship. Teens are very "now" oriented. They are usually focused on what is happening in front of them and have difficulty looking into the future.

Forgiveness is also a critical part of friendship that we must discuss with our teen. Talk about what forgiveness looks like in friendships and how it applies, especially as a Christian. It is also important to remind our teen what forgiveness does not look like. Forgiveness does not mean that our teen must remain in the relationship or maintain contact if they are not comfortable. Forgiveness simply means we must maintain a heart of love as Christ would, and treat the other with respect as God's child. While Jesus loved the Pharisees, they were not his friends. They longed to destroy Him and eventually, they crucified Him. We must remind our teens that there will be "Pharisees" that cross their path. While they can forgive and act with God's love, they can do so at a distance.

Trust is also a crucial part of friendship. Too many teens suffer broken hearts because they allow others to know too much about them too soon or allow others into their hearts too quickly. Compare it to meeting a new dog for the first time. When you meet the dog, he may look cute, cuddly and playful, but it is wise to put your hand out and let him smell you before you hug him. Encourage your teen to give relationships time to build and to test the character and heart of their friend. Asking questions such as the following will be helpful:

- ➢ Am I comfortable with the way my friend talks to me?

- ➢ Is there anything my friend does that causes distrust in my heart?

- ➢ Is my friend hurtful and if so, do they apologize and try to correct the behavior when they recognize they have offended me?

- ➢ Do I feel better about myself when I have been with my friend?

> ➤ Are there any deal-breakers in my friendship - things that I cannot or will not tolerate?

Emotional manipulation may also become a part of our teen's friendship. What if our teen encounters a friend who threatens to end the friendship when their demands are not met? If this happens, remind your teen that some people do not have a "pure heart" where friendships are concerned. Those who use guilt to control others are emotionally manipulating and are not healthy friends. Assure your teen that turning away from such a trait is not only healthy, it is liberating. For example, if Susie says, "I'm not coming to your house until you promise to let me borrow your red shirt," inform your teen that this is emotional manipulation. While such manipulation may seem insignificant, these types of manipulations often grow worse as friendships progress. Emotional manipulation must be confronted and stopped in order to have a healthy friendship.

We must also teach our teen that sharing information with friends is healthy, but sharing it too quickly is a red flag. When teens encounter someone who will "bare their soul" at the first encounter, they should recognize this as a warning sign. Assure your teen that it is okay to walk cautiously when this occurs and remain somewhat distant until they get to know the person better. Friendships are built on trust and while we often "need" our friends, "neediness" will take our teen down a very unhealthy road. It is important that our teen sets clear boundaries in such situations.

When our teens are part of a healthy friendship where they feel respected, valued and supported, they can flourish. When our teen is part of an unhealthy friendship, damage can undo what we have worked hard as parents to instill.

Friendships are built on trust and while we often "need" our friends, "neediness" will take your teen down a very unhealthy road.

There are warning signs we can teach our teen to look for when watching for unhealthy friendships. The following may be helpful:

* One person constantly tries to change the other.

* There are more bad times than good.

* One person makes fun of the other's interests or opinions.

* One throws a tantrum (yells, threatens) and even becomes physical (hits or throws things) when they don't get their way in the friendship.

* One person makes most of the decisions.

* Interests are dropped and other friends are excluded because they are "best" friends.

If your teen's unhealthy friendships begin to affect their performance at school, it is important to address this immediately. A study published in the February 2013 Journal of Early Adolescence showed that friendships can make the difference between good and bad grades. Researchers at the University of Oregon surveyed more than 1,200 middle school students and asked them to identify their three best friends. They found that students whose friends were prone to misbehave didn't do as well in school as kids whose friends were socially active in positive ways (Ulene). As a former school counselor, I have many examples that can prove this point and one particular scenario comes to mind.

After lunch period was over, a teacher ran into my office and frantically announced that five of her students were missing. Calming her, I assured her there must be a logical explanation. As we searched the school, we soon realized the children were not on school grounds. Authorities were notified and my job was to call parents and let them know of their missing children. Needless to say, this was not one of my favorite days on the job.

Parents and authorities immediately arrived at the school, and we began the search for the five missing children. All who were missing were very good friends, so we hoped they would be together.

After an hour of driving through nearby subdivisions, we found the children playing on a neighborhood playground. They didn't seem to have a care in the world until they saw my car pull in to the parking lot.

Suddenly, friends turned into enemies and fingers began pointing.

When we arrived back in my office, parents were waiting and consequences were issued. Each child spent time talking with me about friendship choices and learning to say "No" when peer pressure arises. When asked about their greatest regret, four out of five said, "I got a zero on my spelling test because I wasn't there."

If you notice that your teen's performance in school begins to falter, don't be afraid to have a conversation with your teen about your concerns and the friendships that may be interfering. Without blaming the friend, state how your teen's performance has weakened since the friendship began. Ask your teen how the two might coincide. Be clear and strong as you express your expectations about school performance in the future and hold your teen accountable for their performance. If performance does not improve, consequences must be put into place, so make the punishment fit the crime. If your teen is falling behind in a class, hire a tutor who can work on a weekend evening. Studying with a tutor instead of going out on the weekends may be just the motivation your teen needs to distance themselves from friends who are affecting their grades.

Sometimes our teens find friends who are in abusive situations. Remind your teen that they are not to intervene directly, as this can bring them harm and only make matters worse for their friend. Those who can help in these situations include pastors, youth directors, school counselors, or the Teen Dating Abuse Hotline.

As our teens mature, friendship patterns often change. When our kids are younger, they tend to befriend those who are closest in proximity such as the neighborhood kids or those they see at church. As teenagers mature, however, they usually become more selective about their friends. Teens begin to search out others who have similar interests, values, personalities and beliefs. They will also begin to depend on friends for support, guidance and understanding. While this is often hard for us as parents to understand, remember that it is a natural part of our teen's growth. Don't take it personally. Encourage your teen as they make good decisions selecting friends, and love your teen's friends the way they do.

As I was writing this chapter, I had the privilege of watching a similar scenario unfold. I was visiting a friend who has two daughters. While we sat on the back porch talking, several of the girl's friends came through the back door. Every one of them stopped, hugged my friend, and said something sweet to her. Some of them even called her "Momma." It was obvious that this mom had it figured out. She was so welcoming, and her daughters stayed close to home as a result.

Encourage healthy relationships by welcoming your teen's friends and their parents into your home. When you make your home inviting, "They will come." If you have boys, include some good food and games (pool table, etc.). If you have girls, food is always good, but give them some privacy to sit and talk or watch "chick flicks."

You may also want to invite your teen's friends on family outings. Take them hiking, fishing or shopping with you. Allow your teen to spend quality time with their friend, and quietly observe the interaction.

If you find that time spent with friends begins to override many of the other responsibilities in your teen's life, don't be afraid to set limits. Let your teen know that thirty minutes on the phone per night is all that will be allowed, and then have them put their phone in a common place until the following day. Texting or instant messaging is still part of communication and can be a disruption from the things they need to be doing (homework, chores, etc.). Have a central place where all phones belong after a certain time of night. I recently purchased a "cell jail" which is a little box with a lock on it. If you try to open it after it has been locked, it begins saying, "Step away from the phone." It is a fun way to remind everyone that there are limits on phone usage.

Remember parents, all of our children have different social styles. One child may be a homebody while the other child is never home. Unless your child has a pathological fear of friendships, allow your teen to move at their own pace when developing friendships. The best way we can help our teens with building friendships is to build a strong, Christ-centered identity in our teen. When they know who they are in Christ, they have the greatest chance at finding friendships that will exemplify Proverbs 17:17, "A friend loves at all times."

PARENT PAUSE:

1. What tools will you use to help your teen develop healthy friendships?

2. At what point do you believe a parent should intervene in teen friendship?

3. How can you encourage your teen's healthy friendships? Invite them to dinner? Have them visit your home?

CHAPTER SEVEN

THE BULLIES AMONG US

"Courage is fire, bullying is smoke."
-Benjamin Disraeli

Bullying is the use of force or coercion to abuse or intimidate others and involves a perceived imbalance of power. The victim of bullying is commonly referred to as the "target." Bullying involves various forms of abuse including physical, emotional, mental and verbal attacks. When bullying is inflicted by a group it is called mobbing.

The "perceived imbalance" which prompts bullies to act out is the result of viewing another as weaker. A bully's victim may be smaller in stature, a different race or religion. They may even receive abuse because they're quiet in nature.

At the core, bullies are very insecure individuals who are afraid of being exposed. In order to avoid rejection, bullies find victims who are unlikely to retaliate. Bullies place negative focus on their victim so they appear "better" in the eyes of others. Bullies are very "self-focused" individuals and control drives them.

Many bullies are narcissistic in nature and believe they have the right to treat others any way they choose. Some bullies suffer from mental disorders and need professional help. "It's estimated that 1 out of 4 elementary-school bullies will have a criminal record by the time they are 30" (Lyness).

As a teacher and public school counselor for fourteen years, I witnessed tears, anger, and the gripping fear that bullying produces in its victims. I also witnessed the ultimate devastation that bullying can bring.

Tara was a beautiful, outgoing and sensitive little girl in elementary school. She and I began working together as a result of the bullying taking place in her classroom. Many days she would run to my office in tears because another person had been mean to her or to one of her friends. Tara's sensitivity was a target for bullies. She was kind to everyone and would have never thought of retaliating. Instead, she did what many victims of bullying do. She kept it all inside.

As I began working with Tara and her mom, we found effective ways for Tara to respond to bullies. Tara's self-confidence grew stronger and she learned how to ignore remarks and behavior, as well as respond to a bully when needed. What did not change when I worked with Tara was her sensitivity. It was a beautiful attribute of Tara and the reason she had so many friends.

When Tara left elementary school, I lost contact with her family until the beginning of her junior year in high school. Tara "friended" me on Facebook, and as always, had such kind and sweet words to say. As I read her messages, it was obvious that her personality had not changed in all of those years. Her kind heart was obvious in every word she wrote.

Tara was also successful socially. She was very popular in high school and was a prominent member of the school's dance team. Unfortunately, Tara was still dealing with some "mean girls" in high school and the interactions were more serious than those she encountered during her elementary school days. One particular member of the dance team harassed Tara relentlessly. Tara and her mom contacted the school, but felt little support for the situation that ensued. One October night, Tara decided she could no longer endure the torture. She took a gun and ended her life.

Tara's mother asked if I would speak and sing at her funeral. The enormous sanctuary overflowed with teenagers who came to honor Tara's life. She was so loved, and I couldn't help but wonder if Tara would have made the same decision if she could have seen the love in that room.

As I stepped up to the platform to speak, I looked down to see her grieving mother sitting on the front row. Tara was an only child and was her mother's world since the two of them lived alone. The senseless act of bullying caused such heartbreak that day that watching it was unbearable at times.

Since Tara's death, I have stayed in close contact with her mom. I stand in amazement at the strength she continues to show after Tara's death. Although she is quick to share that her life will never be the same, she is also quick to share her hope in Jesus Christ and her determination to help educate others on the warning signs and effects of bullying. She longs to share the experience of bullying and suicide from a parent's perspective and you can read more from Tara's mom in Appendix A.

Tara's story is not isolated. Over 3.2 million students suffer at the hands of bullies each year ("11 Facts about Bullying").

I know first-hand the terror that can be created by bullies when we feel we have no tools to defend ourselves. Growing up, I was slightly overweight and the children in my neighborhood bullied me continually. There were many times I would run home from playing outside, and ask my mom and dad why I was so "ugly and unloved." I often cried myself to sleep believing the lies of the bullies until the summer I turned 13. I grew several inches in just a few months and when I returned to school for the fall, I wasn't just one of the tallest girls in the school, but also, the thinnest. No one ever made fun of me again, because they had to look up to me. Suddenly, I was considered tall and pretty to my peers, and I became a popular school cheerleader. Unfortunately, those old lies continued playing in my head. "You're ugly, you're worthless and no one wants to be around you," were lies I had exchanged for the truth. Although I was on the honor roll, head cheerleader and even a finalist in beauty pageants, the tapes in my head continued to play. The damage done by those neighborhood bullies was deep. I had difficulty not believing the lies at times. Fortunately, I had parents and friends who spoke the TRUTH of God's word into me, and eventually, I was able to overcome the low self-esteem that bullying had exacerbated.

One out of every 10 students who drops out of school does so because they are bullied.

Bullies can be friends, siblings, acquaintances, dates or even, yes, parents. Bullies can be total strangers, or those who are closest to us. Those who have been bullied often bully in return, while some are so beaten down they never tell anyone.

In order to help our tween and teen deal with bullying, we must know some important facts about bullying.

- The most common reason people are bullied is because of their physical appearance. Two out of five teens feel that they are bullied because of the way that they look ("11 Facts about Bullying").

- One out of every 10 students who drops out of school does so because they are bullied ("11 Facts about Bullying").

- It is estimated that 160,000 children miss school every day due to fear of being bullied ("11 Facts about Bullying").

- One in seven students in Grades K-12 is either a bully or a victim of bullying ("Facts & Statistics").

- 71 percent of students report incidents of bullying as a problem at their school ("Facts & Statistics").

- 282,000 students are physically attacked in secondary schools each month ("Facts & Statistics").

- 90 percent of 4th through 8th graders report being victims of bullying ("Facts & Statistics").

- A victim of bullying is twice as likely to take his or her own life compared to someone who is not a victim ("11 Facts about Bullying").

- 1 in 4 teachers see nothing wrong with bullying and will only intervene 4 percent of the time ("11 Facts about Bullying").

From the statistics above, one can see that it is imperative that both teens and their parents know what to do when bullying occurs. The Bible says, "God has not given us a spirit of fear, but of power, love and a sound mind" (II Timothy 1:7).

The TRUTH of God's Word and strategic steps will help teens and parents confront bullying effectively.

Some suggested steps we can use as parents to confront bullying are listed below:

➤ Teach zero tolerance for any type of bullying behavior in your home. Even when disguised as a "joke," words are hurtful.

➤ Talk with your teen about appropriate ways to handle/display anger.

➤ Teach words of empathy by example, such as "I'm sorry, please forgive me."

➤ Discuss movie scenes or television shows that involve bullying. As a family, discuss the appropriate behavior that should have taken place in bullying situations. It's even happening in cartoons!

➤ If your teen tells you they are being bullied, LISTEN! They need to be heard.

➤ Avoid interrogating words like "Why" and "You." Let your teen feel their feelings and reassure them it is normal to feel hurt, angry, scared or alone when bullied.

➤ Find out if there are more victims by talking with other parents.

➤ Talk to school officials about their anti-bullying policies and procedures. If they do not have one, STRONGLY suggest they develop one.

➤ If your teen is bullied, keep a long, detailed journal of any injuries/incidents that occur, including pictures of injuries.

➤ Help your teen find an adult they can report to on a daily basis while at school.

➤ Monitor your child's whereabouts and friendships.

➤ Watch for signs of anger, anxiety or depression.

➤ Above all, teach your child social skills and how to find the right kind of friends.

If you find that your teen has been the victim of bullying, try to remain calm. When we react by fear or anger, it can make things worse. Some parents I have counseled contact the parents of the bully and let them know their thoughts on the situation before gaining all the facts. This can backfire and cause your tween or teen more harassment. If you feel that you need to contact the parents of the bully, be sure that you discuss it with your teen and make the contact when you are calm. Remember, bullies often breed bullies. If you are dealing with a bully, there is a chance they have witnessed bullying in their home or surrounding environment.

Most importantly, refrain from telling your teen to retaliate, for both spiritual and practical reasons. Refusing to retaliate goes against everything our flesh feels when we are bullied, but we must keep one important reminder in mind: "The bully's modus operandi is to get a reaction." When we react and respond with a firm and Godly response, the bully loses power. Need a scriptural reminder? I Peter 3:9 says, "Do not repay evil for evil or reviling for reviling, but on the contrary, bless, for to this you were called, that you may obtain a blessing." While this verse does not necessarily encourage ongoing relationships with a bully, it does remind us to bless them.

But how can we bless a bully? One way is to give him what he needs – humility. We can help bullies find humility when we refuse to feed the controlling monster that lives inside of them. When we retaliate, cry, carry-on or give in, we meet the needs of the bully and only feed the monster. The control gets worse, and the bully feels new power. As a former school administrator, I will also remind you that under most school policies, your teen becomes as guilty as the bully when they retaliate.

It is likely that the bully's behavior will initially escalate after your teen stands up to the bad behavior of the bully. After all, your teen is challenging the control that the bully desperately seeks. When this occurs, remind your teen to stay safe and to stay strong. If your teen feels they are in physical danger, tell them to move away from the physical space of the bully. If they need support at school to confront the bully, they should ask for it. If bullying takes place outside of the school environment, permit them to contact authorities if the need arises. Remind your teen that their safety comes first, and there are options if they feel unsafe.

When bullying takes place at school and your teen reports it to an adult who does nothing, encourage your teen to go to another adult until intervention takes place. Parents, you and your teen must go as high as you need to go in the administrative chain until someone listens to you. DO NOT STOP going up the ladder of authority until someone addresses the bullying behavior. Never promise your teen that you won't tell anyone about the bullying. Instead, reassure your teen that you will do your best not to make the bullying worse. Let them know you will not give up until the issue is resolved.

DO NOT STOP going up the ladder of authority until someone addresses the bullying behavior.

While many are on the receiving end of bullying, what can you do if YOUR teen IS the bully? The first thing we must do is to remain calm. While this may not be a "normal" reaction, it must be your initial reaction. Next, meet with any adults who may have witnessed your teen's bullying behavior. If there were no adults who can give an account of your teen's behavior, talk calmly with the kids who were involved. Once you have the facts, give clear and appropriate consequences to your teen. Make your teen apologize to those they have offended and be sure to witness the apology.

If your teen continues their bullying behavior, you may need to "shadow" them. When you follow your teen everywhere – whether to school or a party – they will quickly know that you plan to hold them accountable for their behavior toward others. While following your teen, be sure to recognize the positive things they do. If the bullying continues after you "shadow" your teen, get professional help immediately.

When our teen is the victim of bullying, we must fill their toolbox with tools to counter the bully. Some things our teen can say to a bully include the following:

➤ "Say what you want to say. I'm not going to stand here and listen to it." Then, turn around and walk away.

➤ Say "STOP IT" with a reassured and calm look. Remember, bullies are looking for a reaction, so staying calm is VERY important.

➤ Say something like, "This is a waste of my time."

➤ Agreeing with the bully is also a fun way to deflect their insults. For example, if a bully says, "You're fat," say, "You know, you're right; I could stand to lose a few pounds. Thanks for noticing." It throws them off almost every time.

There are also some tools our teens can use to show physical strength in the face of a bully. First, remind your teen to always keep their head up and to look confident. It is important that a bully never see our teen with a hurt or fearful look. Fear and insecurity feed the monster! Our teen may feel fear, but it is important that they do not show it. Bullies can "sniff out fear" and it is like blood to a shark. If your teen struggles to hide their fear, encourage them to "fake it 'til they make it," then talk about their feelings with you or another trusted individual. Remind your teen to keep their arms to their side and to stand on both feet. They must keep their hands out of their pockets since that is a sign of insecurity.

Our teen must also remember to keep non-threatening eye contact with the bully. Threats are enticing to bullies.

Most importantly, insist that your teen never run away from a bully UNLESS they are in PHYSICAL DANGER. Our teen must never get physical or argue with the bully in return. A fight is what a bully wants, and strong repercussions may occur once our teen is embroiled in the brawl. I know a young lady who is very gentle, quiet and soft spoken. She is in no way boisterous, but once she had enough of being bullied, she exchanged punches with the bully. Although the bully threw the first punch, she too was expelled from school for fighting and was forced to serve the same term as the one who had been harassing her. While this seems unfair to some, it is reality in many schools and courtrooms.

We must also encourage our teen to find good, true friends with similar standards when teaching them to avoid bullies. Our teens must know they are safe to share their hurts or disappointments. Friends they deem trustworthy are essential.

Cyberbullying is another form of bullying where technology is used to harass, threaten, embarrass or target another person. This form of bullying may include use of the internet, Facebook, emails, texts, and other technological programs. Cyberbullying is taken very seriously by the law and often involves severe consequences, including the possibility of arrest.

Cyberbullying is common because bullies know they are often more difficult to trace. Cyberbullies believe they may not have to confront their victims so they feel confident hiding behind technology.

The most important thing to teach our teen is NOT to respond to a cyberbully. If they do, there is written evidence of the response and our teen's name may be drawn into controversy.

In order to effectively deal with a cyberbully, have your teen save all evidence of bullying on a flash drive. Once the evidence is saved, it needs to be removed from your teen's technology. Removing evidence of bullying removes the reminder of bullying. Keep the flash drive in a safe place, and then report the bullying to your internet service provider. You must also be sure your teen blocks the bully from sending texts, notes or emails to any of their accounts. Once those accounts are blocked, be sure your teen protects their cell phone and other technology with strong pass-words. Remind your teen to change their password often, and under NO CIRCUMSTANCES should your teen give their password to ANYONE besides you. More teens are exposed to bullying and other forms of negative behavior because they grant access to those who have no business in their personal information.

We want our teens to be safe and they must know they can talk with us about their bullying concerns. If our teen is uncomfortable talking with us, we must find a trusted youth director, friend or other adult who can listen and help give our teen insight into their response to bullying.

If you would like more information about bullying, be sure to visit Appendix B at the back of the book. Included are key points from a curriculum I wrote when working for one of the largest school districts in Texas. Many of the procedures and suggestions are still used today.

PARENT PAUSE:

1. Has your teen ever been a victim of bullying? If so, what steps did you take to handle the situation?

2. If you were a bystander of a bullying situation, what steps would you take to help the victim?

3. Does your teen's school have an anti-bullying policy in place? If so, what are the procedures listed for handling bullying? If not, what can you do to raise awareness that a plan should be implemented?

CHAPTER EIGHT

THE TRAPS OF TECHNOLOGY

"It has become appallingly obvious that our technology has exceeded our humanity."

-Albert Einstein

A recent study shows that today's teens spend more than 7.5 hours per day consuming media (Ahuja). Watching television, listening to music, surfing the web, social networking and playing video games fall under the guise of media. So why should we as parents be alarmed by such a statistic?

According to the Bureau of Labor Statistics' 2011 American Time Use Survey, high school students spent on average less than an hour per weekday on sports, exercise or recreation (Ahuja). With the increasing lack of physical activity, it's not surprising that the percentage of teens that are overweight has more than tripled since 1980. In 2004 almost one in five teens was overweight ("Teen Health"). Staying "plugged in" is not only causing health issues, it also causes emotional concerns since teens who are over-weight usually struggle with lowered self-esteem.

Since 78% of teens have cell phones, any form of media is available at their fingertips ("Teens & Technology 2013"). How can we as parents keep up with the ever-evolving web of technology our teens use on a daily basis? We must become savvy when it comes to social media. We close the gap between our generation and the "iGeneration" by setting limits on social media, and giving guidance to our teens on the proper use of technology.

Since cell phones are the most commonly used devices among teenagers, we must know what is available to our teens at the touch of a finger. Smart phone apps are ever-changing, and while some promote healthy, clean fun, others can be quite dangerous to our tweens and teens.

Instagram is one such app that has potential dangers. Instagram is a photo-sharing app where users follow one another, commenting and "liking" pictures that are posted. It is similar to the basic timeline features on Facebook. While Instagram has an "Over 13" policy, it is easy for tech-savvy teens to get around such limits when signing up. Once teens enter a birth date stating they are over the age of 13, they have an account. There are several cyber risks with Instagram. Once pictures are posted, they are readily available for anyone on the internet to view. To protect your teen, ask them to toggle the "Photos are Private" switch to "ON" from their profile page. Once their page is set to private, anyone who desires to see the photos must send a request asking permission to see the pictures and our teen must approve the request. Our teens must be careful of hitting the "Geotagged" button as well. This allows viewers to see the physical address and location of where the photos are taken. To help provide the greatest protection to your teen, suggest they only allow "followers" on Instagram that they know, and caution them about posting pictures of themselves. This helps to prevent strangers from coming into their very private world.

Private messaging apps include everything from self-destructing messages to coded messages that can only be unscrambled with a code by permission from the sender. The potential cyber risk involves sexting. Teens must remember that nothing stops the recipient of the picture from taking a screen shot of their image before it disappears. Snapchat and KIK are examples of such programs that not only transfer pictures privately, but offer no guarantee that photos will be deleted from their server. It was also noted recently that a flaw with Snapchat security displayed the email address of the sender. Once a recipient enters an email address into Facebook, the sender's profile comes up; therefore, nothing is anonymous about the sender.

KIK is closely tied to Instagram and the Ask account. The KIK app is a messaging system for phones, iPods and iPads. Teens do not need to have phone or texting service to use KIK. When comments on Instagram or Ask say, "KIK me at," or "My KIK name is _____," the viewer is asking to have a private conversation with your teen using an online chat. While comments on Instagram are public, chats on KIK are not and this is where the danger lies. Experts strongly recommend that teens do not download the KIK app for this reason. Private messaging apps are difficult to monitor and teens are easily exploited as a result. Teens are held more accountable when messaging is not private, and according to a recent survey, half of all teens said they would change their online behavior if a parent was watching ("How Teens are Getting Past Parents").

> *Private messaging apps are difficult to monitor and teens are easily exploited as a result.*

MeetMe is also a popular app. This app claims to help teens meet new friends online as well as meet them at local establishments. According to Common Sense Media, MeetMe is the app version of the popular online flirting, entertainment and social networking website formerly called MyYearbook. ("MeetMe – Meet New People") There are definitely privacy and safety concerns. MeetMe is different from Facebook. The primary use of MeetMe is to meet new people and interact with them online rather than keeping up with real-life friends. Teens often pay to put their profile at the top of the homepage of MeetMe as a spotlight for others to see. Their goal is to get "priority in match" to increase the number of secret admirers they get. There are many flirty overtones which could become extremely dangerous if your teen begins visiting local establishments as a result of those they encounter on MeetMe.

BangWithFriends is an app that Facebook offers which allows people to anonymously register an interest to have a sexual encounter with their Facebook contacts. If their interest is not reciprocated, it remains a secret. If the other party has also ticked the box to show their interest, both are made aware and the user's "Down to Bang" button changes to say "Awaiting Bang." Facebook claims that there is an average of five new registrations per minute. While the dangers are obvious, users of BangWithFriends may not realize that anyone can see their "bang" status. Once a user goes in to find a friend, they can type in the words "friends interested in sex" and with a thorough search, find friends who are part of BangWithFriends.

Omegle is another app used for talking to strangers via online chat. The service randomly pairs up users online into one-on-one chat sessions where they chat anonymously using the handles "You" and "Stranger" ("What is Omegle"). Its logo contains an omega (Ω) turned diagonally. The chat service includes anonymous chat, stranger chat, or one-on-one chat and allows the user to chat via text or video. The Omegle homepage clearly states that the service is not for those under 13 and that those under 18 must have their parent's permission – although there is nothing stopping them from downloading the app without it. Users can also connect Omegle to their Facebook page and Facebook will attempt to pair chat partners with similar interests. Once Omegle is connected to your teen's Facebook page, Facebook friends could potentially see Omegle activity on your teen's profile. Teens can change that setting to "Me Only" so that Omegle activity is not shared.

The Omegle privacy policy makes it very clear to their users that all information is saved on their servers for 120 days. At the time the chat begins, your teen's IP address and other information are saved on Omegle's server. At the end of an Omegle chat, users have the option to save the chat's log and share the link. Your teen's conversation is not really private and the contents of the chat, including any personal information they might share, can be sent to anyone without their knowledge.

To find out if your teen is using Omegle, take a look at the history in their web browser. Just as any other site your teen visits, it is stored as part of their browsing history unless they have deleted it. A more simple way to find out is to ask your teen about any of their online or app uses.

In order to be aware of all your teen's social interactions, it is imperative that you are a member of every account in which your teen participates. While you may never use the social media sites personally, you will be able to monitor any and all activity.

Many programs are offered to help aid parents in the restriction of online services to their teens. While no filtering software on a PC, mobile phone or laptop is 100% effective, there are many offered which help teens stay safe in cyber world. When considering parental control software, remind your teen that you are doing so for their safety. Remind them that any information they share in cyberspace may also be used for cyberbullying or may be misconstrued to embarrass them later in life.

According to NetSafe, the following are parental control software suggestions for cellular phones:

➢ Android phones
  • Android Parental Controls app (Free)
  • Phone Control (Free)
  • Vodafone Guardian (Free for Vodafone NZ Prepay and On Account plans)

➢ Apple iOS – iPhone, iPod Touch
  • McAfee Family Protection (US$19.99)
  • iOS Settings (Free – built in)
  • Advice on Apple Parental Controls for iPad

➢ Symbian (Nokia phones)
  • SMobile Security Shield Parental Controls Edition

- ➤ Windows Mobile 7
  - Mobile Parental Controls
    ("How Can I")

Free Parental controls for PC's, laptops and iPads are also available and include the following:

- Norton Online Family
- Windows Live Family Safety
- Family Safety Parental Controls Software
- PG Surfer
- K9 Web Protection

Browser add-ons such as BlockSite for Firefox and Chrome are also available.

Microsoft Windows and Apple Computers provide access to parental controls, as do many gaming systems and digital television services. These controls help parents manage time teens spend on their computer, programs they run, and games they play. They also control access to websites visited. Parental control systems provide "activity reports" for parents that include a list of most recent websites visited, recent websites blocked, files downloaded and more.

Many parents come to me for advice when worried their teen will think they don't trust them if parental controls are put in place. I always remind parents that trust is earned, and as the parent, it is our responsibility to make sure our teen is safe at all times. When teens struggle with the thought of having parental devices on their technology, I strongly suggest that parents share stories to illustrate safety concerns. One story you may tell your teen is about Peter Chapman, a registered sex offender who was sentenced to life in prison for kidnapping, raping and murdering Ashleigh Hall, 17. Chapman courted and lured Hall to her death using Facebook (Smith). You may also share the story of 15-year-old Audrie Pott, who hanged herself after she was "savagely assaulted by her fellow high school students." Her aggressors shared cell phone photos of the attack with 1,400 students at her high school. Tell your teen how social media-related crime has increased 780% in four years ("Social Media-related"). After sharing these statistics, remind your teen you are suggesting parental control and oversight because you love them and are concerned for their safety, and that statistics show you have good reason to do so.

We must also be careful about sharing credit card information with our teens. Occasionally, our teen's friends may have access to our computers. While innocently working on a PC in our home, it is easy to view or use credit card information when it is stored. I-Tunes accounts host your credit card, as well as many gaming apps, so be sure to turn off "in app" purchasing so that others have no access to purchase content from the application.

Most parents struggle with "how much is enough" where social media, technology and cell phones are concerned. A contract is effective and may be signed between you and your teen as a reminder that there are rules which must be followed. Following are suggestions that may be used when designing an agreement regarding cell phone usage.

Cell Phone Contract: Child Responsibility

I will not send threatening or mean texts to others.

I will not text or place phone calls after 9 p.m.

I will keep my phone charged at all times.

I will not bring my cell phone to the family dinner table.

I will not go over our plan's monthly minutes or text message limits. If I do, I understand that I may be responsible for paying any additional charges or that I may lose my cell phone privileges.

I understand that I am responsible for knowing where my phone is, and for keeping it in good condition.

I understand that my cell phone may be taken away if I talk back to my parents, fail to do my chores, or I fail to keep my grades up.

I will obey rules of etiquette regarding cell phones in public places. I will make sure my phone is turned off when I am in church, in restaurants, or quiet settings.

I will obey any rules my school has regarding cell phones, such as turning them off during class, or keeping them on vibrate while riding the school bus.

I promise I will alert my parents when I receive suspicious or alarming phone calls or text messages from people I don't know.

I will also alert my parents if I am being harassed by someone via my cell phone.

I will not use my cell phone to bully another person.

I will send no more than _____ texts per day.

I understand that having a cell phone can be helpful in an

emergency, but I know I must still practice good judgment and make good choices that will keep me out of trouble or out of danger.

I will not send embarrassing photos of my family or friends to others. In addition, I will not use my phone's camera to take embarrassing photos of myself or others.

I understand that having a cell phone is a privilege, and if I fail to adhere to this contract, my cell phone privilege may be revoked.

Cell Phone Contract: Parent Responsibilities

I will make myself available to answer any questions my teen might have about owning a cell phone and using it responsibly.

I will support my teen when he or she alerts me to an alarming message or text message they have received.

I will alert my teen if our cell phone's plan changes and impacts the plan's minutes.

I will give my teen _____ warning(s) before I take his or her cell phone away.

Signed _____ (Teen)

Signed _____ (Parents)

Date _____

(O'Donnell)

Parents do not be afraid to give your teen consequences if your rules about social media are not followed. Teens value their connection with their friends, and they will be much

Parents do not be afraid to give your teen consequences if your rules about social media are not followed.

more likely to abide by your standards regarding social media if they know you will enforce removing the phone.

You must also implement times when teens are away from their phones. Dinner time is a good time to "unplug." Give your teen a time to turn in their cell phone each night. Another boundary I STRONGLY suggest is not allowing your teen to sleep with their cell phone. Sleep patterns may be disturbed, and your teen needs time to decompress from a constant influx of information.

While we have explored many negative sides of technology, we know there is definitely an upside – for teens AND for parents. A clinical report from the American Academy of Pediatrics revealed the positive use for social media, including:

* Connect with people with shared interests
* Learn about people with varied backgrounds
* Enhance creativity by sharing musical and artistic projects
* Expand ideas by creating blogs, videos, and podcasts
* Collaborate on school projects outside of class
* Raise money for charity
* Volunteer for local charitable and political events (O'Keeffe)

Many websites are available which help educate parents on positive and negative effects of social media, and do so from a Christian perspective. Parents, take the time to do your homework. Enter the words "social media, parents, educate, Christian" in your internet browser and you will find many websites willing to help you learn the latest in social media trends.

The dialogue you have about technology with your teen will be ongoing. Ephesians 4:29 reminds us to "Let no corrupt communication proceed out of our mouth, but that which is good to the use of edifying, that it may minister grace unto the hearers." There is no better place for our teens to put this scripture into practice than with social media. Ask God to direct you and to reveal TRUTH to you and your teen in the use of social media.

PARENT PAUSE:

1. What apps or programs have you found most challenging while raising your teen?

2. What have you found are the most effective ways to deal with the challenges technology offers while raising a teen?

3. What resources have you found are most helpful in keeping up with the ever-changing world of technology? How will you discuss these new trends and the concerns that they may bring with your teen?

CHAPTER NINE

DRINKING, DRUGS, AND "OTC'S"

"Wine is a mocker and beer a brawler; whoever is led astray by them is not wise."

-Proverbs 20:1

There is nothing that breaks the heart of a parent more than finding out their teen is experimenting with or addicted to alcohol, drugs or other mind-altering substances. Experimentation opens doors to habit. Habit opens doors to addiction. Unfortunately, we do not know how substances will affect our teen until it is often too late. When open communication is available, parents can intervene with love and potentially save their teen from following a dangerous road.

According to Discovery Health:

> There are more deaths and disabilities each year in the U.S. from substance abuse than from any other cause. About 18 million Americans have alcohol problems and approximately 5 to 6 million Americans have drug problems. More than half of all adults have a family history of alcoholism or problem drinking, and more than nine million children live with a parent dependent on alcohol and/or il-

legal drugs. One-third of all suicides and more than half of all homicides and incidents of domestic violence are alcohol-related. Almost half of all traffic fatalities are alcohol-related. Between 48% and 64% of people who die in fires have blood alcohol levels indicating intoxication. Fetal alcohol syndrome is the leading known cause of mental retardation.

Alcohol and drug abuse costs the American economy an estimated $276 billion per year in lost productivity, health care expenditures, crime, motor vehicle crashes and other conditions. Untreated addiction is more expensive than heart disease, diabetes and cancer combined… ("Facts about Addiction")

In short…WE HAVE A PROBLEM.

While addiction is no respecter of persons, we must know the warning signs which may make teens more susceptible to addiction. According to Help Guide, the following risk factors increase the vulnerability to addiction in your teen:

*   Family history of addiction

*   Abuse, neglect, or other traumatic experiences in childhood

*   Mental disorders such as anxiety or depression

*   Early use of drugs

*   Method of administration - smoking or injecting a drug may increase addictive potential ("Drug Abuse and Addiction")

So how do the seeds of addiction begin? Simple – the "feel good" sensation. Teens begin experimenting with substances because they experience a release. Some teens prefer to drink or do drugs because it provides a release from the "bad rap" they will receive from friends if they don't experiment. Some teens don't feel pressured, but simply enjoy the release they feel as a result of using substances. Unfortunately, some parents turn a blind eye, believing their teen's experimentation is a phase, and later find their teen has developed an addiction. The longer an addiction is allowed to continue, the more difficult it is to treat; therefore, if you see signs of drug, alcohol or foreign substance abuse in your teen, it is important that action is taken immediately.

Alcohol is the number one abused substance by teenagers in the United States, and underage drinkers account for 11.4% of all the alcohol consumed. The National Clearinghouse for Alcohol and Drug Information reports that there are 3 million teens suffering from full-blown alcoholism. That number does not include the millions more that have an unmanageable drinking problem. Studies conducted by the National Institute on Alcohol Abuse and Alcoholism reveal that 51.7% of eighth graders have tried alcohol, while 25.1% have been drunk and 15.2% have had one or more binge drinking episodes. Of the tenth graders studied, 70.6% have tried alcohol, 48.9% have been drunk and 25.6% have had one or more binge drinking episodes. Binge drinking poses huge concern for students in high school and college. Not only are binge drinkers at greater risk of having a stroke or sudden death, teens are literally drinking themselves to death in just a matter of hours. Twelfth graders show the highest use of alcohol as 80% reported having tried alcohol, 62.3% have been drunk and 30.8 % have had one or more binge drinking episodes. Lastly, 3.6% of twelfth graders claim they use alcohol daily ("Teen Alcohol").

The teen body can be severely affected by alcohol, so we must know the concerns in order to approach our teens with facts. Alcohol is classified as a depressant, so it has the ability to damage the body and the brain. Depressants relax muscles and affect nerves, so alcohol affects every part of our teen's central nervous system. It also affects their cardiovascular system. Alcohol increases the heart rate, which can lead to dizziness, headache and tremors. The effects of alcohol on the brain lead to problems with coordination, balance and vision. Alcohol saturates the part of the brain which helps a person with fine motor skills, reflexes and vision. Alcohol also lowers inhibitions, and alters judgment and reasoning as the cerebral cortex is affected. The cerebral cortex is where thinking and logic take place. The limbic system is also suppressed by alcohol and often creates memory loss as well as high states of emotion when intoxicated. The digestive system is affected as alcohol leads to an increase in acid levels in the stomach. When the stomach and intestines become irritated, some drinkers throw up or have diarrhea. Weight gain is also common as the fermented sugar in alcohol turns to fat in the body.

While the above effects happen in everyone who drinks, some cases are extreme and may cause a coma or even death. Car accidents, alcohol poisoning, falls or other incidences relating to alcohol-induced events are often reported. Did you know that The National Institute on Alcohol Abuse and Alcoholism reports that 50,000 college students in the United States under the age of 21 experience alcohol-related date rape each year, and that 430,000 teens under the age of 21 are assaulted by another student who has been drinking ("Teen Alcohol")? Unprotected sex, an increase in STDs and unwanted pregnancies are also a result of alcohol abuse. Parents, we can keep our teen from being a statistic, but how do we do it?

When talking with your teen about drinking, present the TRUTH. What does the Bible say about alcohol? While some denominations feel alcohol is a stumbling block in our relationship with Christ, others permit the use of alcohol on a moderate basis.

Whatever your belief, God's Word has plenty to say about the abuse of alcohol. Ephesians 5:18 (NLT) says, "Don't be drunk with wine, because that will ruin your life. Instead, let the Holy Spirit fill and control you." I Corinthians 6:10 (ESV) adds, "Nor thieves, nor the greedy, nor drunkards, nor revilers, nor swindlers will inherit the kingdom of God." Additional verses are Proverbs 20:1, I Corinthians 5:11 and Galatians 5:21. All verses warn not only against the sin of being drunk, but the association with drunkards.

I have been told by many parents that they allowed their kids to drink at home so it would take the "unknown" element out of alcohol. I simply asked parents this question, "Are you also allowing your teen to experiment with illegal drugs so that the same occurs?" Parents look stunned, but I believe this is a valid point to consider. When parents provide alcohol for teens and their under-aged friends, it is not only illegal; it can land you in jail. A more important question is, "Am I training my child in the way he/she should go?" Allowing our teens to drink at home does not teach them responsibility. It teaches them that we reinforce their right to drink, wherever they may go. Believing that we can bribe our teens to drink at home so that "we can keep an eye on them" is believing a lie. When teens want to drink, and believe they have our endorsement, they will drink, at home or elsewhere. Our teens are receiving enough encouragement to drink outside of the home. Why not make your home different?

Remind your teen that the legal age for consuming alcohol is 21 for a reason. Teen bodies and brains are simply not developed enough to make good decisions about alcohol consumption – and some are not ready to make good decisions at 21!

In order to prepare your teen for the peer pressure surrounding the use of alcohol, talk with them about the facts. Teach your teen the TRUTH of God's Word and give them tools to walk away from temptation.

One tool we can offer our teen is the option of simply saying, "No!" Parents, "NO" is a complete sentence. While peers may exclude your teen from activities, there are others who don't drink and

Parents, "NO" is a complete sentence.

will befriend your teen. If your teen has friends who drink, remind your teen that true friends respect boundaries. Your teen's friends who choose to drink should respect their decision to abstain from alcohol.

Throughout my life I have chosen to abstain from the use of alcohol. I have been touched by great tragedy as alcohol has affected those I deeply love. I have seen wrecks, arrests, adultery and death as a result of the abuse of alcohol. I even witnessed a case where the FBI got involved and watched the ravaging effects on parents of an addicted teen. I decided at a very young age that I would choose to abstain. My choice was always challenged in both high school and college when I attended events where alcohol was offered. Oddly enough, my refusal of alcohol became a topic of conversation many times. "You don't drink?" some would ask in shock. Friends of mine who did drink often responded, "No, she doesn't, so leave her alone." It was as if they were protecting something they valued and wished they had in their own lives.

Perhaps peer pressure is backing your teen into a corner and they don't feel they have the tools to refuse alcohol. If saying "No" has not been enough, offer these tools to help your teen reject alcohol:

➤ Avoid areas or parties where alcohol will be served.

➤ Make friends with people who do not drink. If alcohol may be an issue at a function, attend the function with others who are non-drinkers.

➤ If someone pressures you to drink, remind them you are driving and that you do not drink and drive.

➤ Tell the one offering alcohol, "I've never acquired a taste for it."

Talk with your teen about your expectations and rules regarding alcohol use. Let your teen know there are consequences for breaking those rules and be willing to enforce those consequences. Be sure your teen understands how you feel about underage drinking, but never scold, nag or complain. This will cause your teen to turn elsewhere to discuss alcohol. Keep the lines of communication open. You must also make it clear that drinking and driving or riding with someone who has been drinking will not be tolerated. Give your teen permission to call for a ride, take a cab, or call for permission to stay overnight if your teen, or a friend who is driving, has been drinking. While this is NOT a license to drink, it reminds your teen that your utmost concern is their safety. Most importantly, be a role model to your teen in the area of drinking. We are responsible for instilling values in our teen, and drinking alcohol is a crucial area where we must take responsibility for how our teen lives his/her life.

If you feel your teen is abusing alcohol, be sure to get help for him/her immediately. Remember, alcoholism is a progressive disease. According to Live Strong the following are signs that your teen is abusing alcohol and needs help:

* Craving alcohol - teen finds ways and excuses to drink at the cost of friendships and commitments

* Unable to stop drinking once they begin

* Guilt over drinking - teens may recognize they have a problem but feel guilty because they can't stop

* Become defensive when confronted about their use of alcohol

* Drinking alone or before a social event

* Binge drinking - consuming a large amount of alcohol at one time for a certain period of time ("Alcohol Abuse Symptoms")

Illegal and over the counter (OTC) drugs are also causing massive concern for parents of teens.

DoSomething.com reports:

> More teens die from prescription drugs than hero-in/cocaine combined and more than 60 percent of teens said that drugs were sold, used, or kept at their school. One in nine high school seniors has tried Spice/K2 (synthetic marijuana) and 1.3 percent of seniors have used bath salts. Bath salts are the informal "street name" for a family of designer drugs which effects mimic that of amphetamines and cocaine. Young people who drink alcohol are 50 times more likely to use cocaine than teens who never drink. Approximately 64 percent of teens surveyed who have abused pain relievers say they got them from friends or relatives. ("11 Facts about Teens and Drug Abuse")

OTC drugs are very popular among teens. Fifty-six percent of teens feel that getting OTC drugs is easier than getting illegal drugs ("OTC Abuse"). Internet accessibility to information about how to get high on OTC drugs, and how to order them, makes over the counter drugs even easier to obtain and use. Most teens are aware that they can "find a high" in their very own bathroom by using cough syrup and other over the counter medications.

What is startling to most parents is finding that a majority of teens are unaware of the dangers of over the counter drugs. Many teenagers I have counseled believe that OTC drugs must be "safe" because they are easily accessible. Cough medicines, diet pills, allergy medications, pain relievers and even sexual enhancement drugs are all being used by teens to get a "buzz."

OTC drugs... are becoming very popular as recreational drugs abused by teens.

OTC drugs, especially cough and cold medications, are becoming very popular as recreational drugs abused by teens ("Most Commonly Used OTC Drugs"). Cold medicines such as Robitussin, Nyquil, Vicks Formula 44, and Coricidin HBP Cough and Cold tablets contain a chemical called Dextromethorphan (DXM), which is found in more than 120 non-prescription cough and cold medications. Teenagers have various nicknames for DXM that parents should be aware of including: Robo, Skittles, Triple C's, Dex, Vitamin D, and Tussin. Coricidin HBP Cough and Cold tablets contain much more potent doses of DXM than cough syrups, so teens can take a few pills containing DXM to get high. DXM is a synthetic drug that is chemically similar to morphine and has been added to cough syrups and some cold medications since the 1970's. Authorities say that DXM overdoses typically occur in clusters of teens, as word of mouth about the drug spreads through middle school and high school-aged teens. Teens also prefer DXM because it is available for just a few dollars. Unfortunately, there is a great deal of information on the Internet regarding how much

DXM it takes to get high, so teens have all the information they need at the touch of their fingertips.

DXM can be very dangerous if misused and there are no legal restrictions on purchasing the drug. While drug manufacturers show concerns about the abuse of DXM, there have been no restrictions placed on consumers. As concern grows, some store chains have restricted access to products containing DXM and have put limits on the number of products that can be purchased at one time.

Motion sickness pills such as Dramamine are being used by teens as OTC drugs and when taken in large doses (one entire package or more) can cause hallucinations. Sleep aids such as Tylenol PM, Excedrin PM, and Sominex are also used by teens to receive a stimulant effect. Energy drinks and drugs such as nasal decongestants containing Pseudoephedrine are also being used to receive a "stimulant" effect while herbal ecstasy is used to achieve euphoria.

Herbal ecstasy is a combination of inexpensive herbs that are legally sold in pill form and swallowed, snorted, or smoked to produce euphoria, increased awareness, and enhanced sexual sensations. The main ingredient in herbal ecstasy is ma huang (Ephedra), an herb banned in the U.S. except in dietary supplements. Ma huang can be purchased in gas stations, health food stores, drug stores, music stores, nightclubs and online. Many teens overdose on herbal ecstasy because the dose needed to achieve certain effects varies. Some teens using herbal ecstasy have severe reactions including increased blood pressure, seizures, heart attacks, strokes and death. Other herbal products are being used by teens because they are difficult to find in drug screenings. Salvia, which is ingested or smoked, produces hallucinations. Nutmeg, eaten as a paste, helps teens experience euphoria and hallucinations. Many side effects can occur from using either product including nausea, vomiting, blurred vision, low blood pressure or rapid heart rate.

Prescription drugs are also a growing "party drug" among teens. In fact, it has recently been confirmed that one in four teens has misused or abused a prescription drug at least once in their lifetime – a 33 percent increase over the past five years (Goldburg).

The Foundation for a Drug Free World reports:

> Every day in the United States, 2,500 youth (12 to 17) abuse a prescription pain reliever for the first time… In the U.S. alone, more than 15 million people abuse prescription drugs, more than the combined number of people who are reported as having abused cocaine, hallucinogens, inhalants and heroin.

> Prescription drug abuse is responsible for the largest amount of drug overdoses… In 2005, 4.4 million teenagers (aged 12 to 17) in the U.S. admitted to taking prescription painkillers, and 2.3 million took a prescription stimulant such as Ritalin. Over two million teens abused over-the-counter drugs

such as cough syrup. The average age for first-time users is now 13 to 14.

According to The National Center on Addiction and Substance Abuse at Columbia University, teens who abuse prescription drugs are twice as likely to use alcohol, five times more likely to use marijuana, and twelve to twenty times more likely to use illegal street drugs such as heroin, ecstasy and cocaine than teens who do not abuse prescription drugs. ("International Statistics")

The most commonly abused prescription drugs are the stimulant Adderall and the pain reliever Vicodin.

Illegal drug use among teens is alarming. According to the National Institute on Drug Abuse, 6.5 percent of 8th graders, 17.0 percent of 10th graders, and 22.9 percent of 12th graders used marijuana in 2012. ("Drug Facts") The rising use of marijuana is believed to be the result of changing attitudes about the drug. As studies advocate the use of marijuana for "medicinal purposes," teens are showing a decreased concern that marijuana is dangerous. However, in most states, marijuana is a Class I substance under the Controlled Substances Act. Marijuana is a controlled substance and those who obtain it illegally will be arrested. Physical dangers of marijuana use include lung disease, memory problems and addiction. Synthetic marijuana, also known as "Spice" or "K2," refers to herbal mixtures and presents the same dangers as THC, the active ingredient in marijuana.

Teens often find access to other illegal drugs including Methamphetamine (meth), Crack, Cocaine, LSD, Heroin, tranquilizers, sedatives, hallucinogens and inhalants. Hallucinogens change a person's perception or reality and cause things to seem like an illusion. PCP, LSD, DMT, Foxy, Psilocybin and mescaline are all forms of hallucinogens. Over one fourth of teens got their drugs from someone on school grounds ("Teens and Illicit Drugs").

Club drugs stimulate teens and produce psychedelic effects at the same time. When drugs are enhanced by music and lights at a "rave," the effects can seem especially exciting. Club drugs used by teens include Ecstasy (MDMA), Rohypnol (a.k.a. the "date rape drug"), GHB and ketamine. Club drugs are popular for use at parties, and become a denial mechanism for teens who mistakenly believe they don't have a drug problem since they only do drugs at parties.

Inhalants may also be used by teens to experience an altering effect. Some inhalants often used by teens include paint thinners and removers, white out, felt-tip markers, aerosol sprays (such as spray paint, hair spray and even vegetable oil sprays), nitrates and gases (such as gasoline, propane and refrigerants).

One of the most difficult cases I encountered as a counselor was working with a young lady who was addicted to illegal and OTC drugs, as well as alcohol. One day while her parents were working, she sold most everything in her parent's home in exchange for her next "high." From electronics to her father's guns, she managed to get enough drugs to last for a while. Fortunately, she didn't have the opportunity to use them. Her parents responded with tough love and contacted authorities. She was arrested and taken to jail. Upon release from jail, she was admitted to drug rehab and she emerged "clean and sober." Her parents said it was the hardest thing they ever did, but it was the right thing to do. Tough love saved their daughter's life.

While cigarette smoking has declined among teens according to studies at the University of Michigan, "hookah" has become a popular way of smoking among teens. (Wadley) A hookah is a water pipe with a smoke chamber, a bowl, a pipe and a hose. Specially made tobacco is heated, and the smoke passes through water and is then drawn through a rubber hose to a mouthpiece. The tobacco used to smoke a hookah pipe is just as toxic as cigarettes. In reality, hookah smokers may actually inhale more tobacco smoke than cigarette smokers do because of the amount of smoke they inhale in one smoking session. Smoking sessions of a hookah pipe can last as long as 60 minutes. Studies from the Americans for Nonsmokers' Rights (ANR) say inhaling smoke from a hookah contains the same carcinogenic components found in cigarette smoke. The ANR also claim that hookah smoke contains more tar than cigarette smoke, eleven times more carbon monoxide and higher levels of lead, nickel and arsenic. In addition, hookah smoke contains nicotine, a chemical found in tobacco leaves that cause an addictive effect ("Hookah Bars").

Using hookahs can increase a person's risk for developing cancer, heart disease and dental disease. Hookah smokers also risk causing damage to their lungs, catching the flu, developing a cold or even catching infections such as oral herpes. Hookahs are shared by many people, which increase the risk of catching viral or bacterial infections. The use of hookah pipes and small cigars continues to be a great health concern among medical professionals.

As if all these statistics are not overwhelming enough to parents, new drugs are frequently made available. So what do we do as parents when we find our teen is experimenting with drugs?

Family Life suggests some strategies for the conversation that will need to take place. First, we must remain calm. The goal is to find out why our teen is doing drugs and to what effect. When we lose our temper, everyone loses. Next, don't blame yourself. This is not a healthy time to begrudge your parenting abilities. Ask other parents for advice who may have experienced a similar situation. Talking with those who have experience in dealing with teens and drugs can give great insight into "what and what not" to do. Finally, let the other family members know what is going on and reassure them you are there for them. It is easy to focus all of our attention on the issue at hand and forget others. (Family Life)

Family Life continues to suggest creating the right environment to talk with your teen about their drug use. Find a place where your teen feels comfortable. Choose a time that is good for both you and your teen to talk. Next, ask open-ended questions such as, "How would you feel if you were in my shoes?" or "How can I help you?" Also, be sure not to negatively label your teen. Telling them they are "stupid" or "a failure" will backfire. Finally, act as a coach. Remind your teen that there are ways for dealing with the issue, and that you are there to help. Your teen needs to know that you will not withdraw your love just because you are disappointed in their choices. (Williams)

Keep in mind that there is no guarantee that your teen will agree to the discussion. In order to be proactive, have others present to help support you. A spouse or close family friend would be helpful. Accountability produces action. Remind your teen that there will be consequences put into place, and if they leave the house, you may have no other choice than to call authorities. If you do call authorities, remind your teen that they may be arrested and if so, they will be drug tested. While this sounds harsh, saving your teen's life is where tough love begins. There is NO more difficult place in this counselor's opinion than dealing with addiction. Why? Because you are fighting a substance, not your teen. When substance abuse is involved, your teen's thoughts, mindset and attitudes are altered. As a result, you must be tough when dealing with drug use. There is no time to wait when teens are experimenting with drugs. Put a stop to it – immediately.

But what if my teen refuses to stop? This is where it gets really difficult. When teens continue using, we must hold them accountable. Let your teen know that you will take them for sporadic drug tests. If you find the drug tests are positive, enroll them in counseling immediate-ly. If your teen refuses to attend counseling, let them know that a rehab program will be the next step. Unfor-tunately, I have counseled parents whose teens have left home to pursue their use of drugs. If your teen is under the age of 18, you may have the authorities return them to your home. If your teen is over 18, this is a heart-wrenching experience for parents, but one that is out of your control. Pray for your teen, and allow God to intervene in ways that only He can. When you have done all that you can do as a parent, it is often the most difficult act of love – letting go – that draws our teen back to our family and to God.

Pray for your teen, and allow God to intervene in ways that only He can.

You may also wish to join a Celebrate Recovery® group. These groups use eight steps for helping others face addiction by using scriptural principles. To find a program near you, type CelebrateRecovery.com in your internet browser's search engine and enter your zip code in the Group Locator menu. When attending a meeting, you will hear from other parents, family members and those struggling with addiction. By attending meetings, you will find healing, hope and help to face addiction. Celebrate Recovery® is self-supporting, so while you may choose to donate after attending a meeting, there is no charge for attendance.

Remember, there are no perfect parents, and there are no guarantees. Some parents who make every effort to instill positive, Godly virtues and values in their teen still face the crushing pain of watching their teen reject those principles. While we may not have control over every choice our teen makes, their Creator, our Heavenly Father, knows just how to call them back home. Our children were His children first and He knows how to handle even the most difficult of situations.

PARENT PAUSE:

1. How will you talk with your teen about alcohol and drugs and the complications they can bring?

2. What can you do to help your home be a healthy environment in the area of alcohol and drugs?

3. Is there anything that needs to change in your life as the parent to help your teen in this area?

CHAPTER TEN

COMMUNICATION, MOTIVATION, AND SELF-ESTEEM

"If you have nothing to say, say nothing"
-Mark Twain

As parents, we long to build strong lines of communication with our teens. So why do we find it so difficult?

As teens mature, their need for communication may not change, but their styles often do. Teens move from total dependence when they were younger to demonstrating independence as they mature. For parents, the changes that occur can be frustrating unless we learn how to adjust with their shifting needs. Moms and Dads often respond differently as the adjustments occur. While moms may INSIST on communicating with their teen, Dads often become quiet or ignore their teen's behavior. Neither is healthy.

I recommend a few strategies to keep the lines of communication open and vibrant. First, learn the art of asking open-ended questions so your teen must give longer than one-word answers. For example, "Tell me some good things that happened in your day today" is much better than asking, "How was your day?" We all know the standard answer to that question – "Fine." Instead of asking "What did you do at school today?" ask, "Tell me three things that you remember learning at school today." These statements let teens know they are accountable for their part of the conversation. "Nothing" is no longer an acceptable answer when asked what they did at school for eight hours.

Secondly, we must respect our teen's decision to allow our input into their conversation. Too many times it is tempting to give our advice when we hear teens talking with one another. When silent, we are more likely to be invited to enter their conversation. When we continually give our opinion, we not only keep our teen from soliciting our opinion, but we go against scripture. Proverbs 18:2 says, "Fools find no pleasure in understanding, but delight in airing their own opinions." Never assume that your teen wants your opinion. If it involves their safety, or morality, most definitely involve yourself in the conversation. Otherwise, wait to be invited.

We must also learn how to control our temper when we are upset with our teen. While often easier said than done, scripture says this is good parenting. Proverbs 15:1 (KJV) reminds us that, "A soft answer turns away wrath: but grievous words stir up anger." Have you had a verbal brawl with your teen lately? If so, you know this verse is true. It takes one bad mood, one wrong word, one harsh tone or one angry look to begin an argument. So what do we do when our tempers are running short, our teen is acting crazy and we are at our wit's end? When you feel you are losing your cool with your teen, remember that angry words can greatly damage relationships. The goal is to keep the lines of communication open with your teen, whatever the cost. If this means you must control the words that come out of your mouth, do it – even if you feel justified in saying what you would like to say. Remember, WE are the ADULTS in the relationship. There can only be one teenager, and we don't get to be it. We are setting the example and angry words are in no way helpful when talking with our teen.

When you find anger building, remember the acronym S.T.O.P. S.T.O.P. stands for "Stop Trouble Offer Patience." You don't have to say it out loud, but quickly say it to yourself to avoid your thoughts and behavior from spinning out of control. While saying something harsh might feel good for the short-term, those same words will put a wedge between you and your teen. Remember, your goal is to keep the lines of communication open so that issues can be resolved.

After you calm down, ask yourself some questions. "Why am I so angry? Is this my child's problem, or is part of the anger my problem? Is one or both of us tired?" There are many factors that can spur disagreements, so we must look for ways to diffuse anger. One way we can diffuse anger is by admitting when we are wrong. Too many parents use the excuse, "Because I'm the parent" to relieve their guilt for damage done during an argument. Once we admit we have blown it, teens will have greater respect for us, and there is a much greater chance that the issue will be resolved.

There are many factors that can spur disagreements, so we must look for ways to diffuse anger.

If you find your anger is justified but you are afraid of losing control, remove yourself physically from the presence of your teen. If you have to physically leave a location for a while, do so. Whatever it takes, let the teen know, "I am angry, but I am not talking with you until I have peace about what I want to say."

Many times teens do things that justify parent's anger. Although our anger is justified, we must NEVER physically strike our teen when angry. Not only does this result in physical danger if our teen retaliates, but it does deep damage to the relationship that may take years to repair. I have seen this happen and it is not an easy fix once it occurs. While the Bible supports "the rod," it never supports doing so when tempers flare or rage is present. Spanking our children when they are small can be effective. As they grow older, talking with them and giving appropriate consequences will much more likely get their attention.

When I was a school counselor, a twelve-year-old boy reported that his father hit him with his fists whenever the child talked in their home. It was the father's belief that "children were meant to be seen and not heard." The abuse was heartbreaking and I was forced to report several of the incidences to Child Protective Services. One day, I got an unannounced visit from daddy. He let me know that I would be the next one to receive his beatings if I interfered in the discipline of his child. He was one of the angriest men I had ever met. I particularly remember how he banged on my desk every time he made a point. To say my heart jumped would be an understatement, but I never let him know it. As his tirade continued, I became distracted by the tattoo of the naked lady that bounced up and down on his arm each time he struck my desk. I tried not to stare, but it took me a while to figure out what it was because his arm moved so fast. Fortunately, my focus on the tattoo kept me from hearing the vile words he was spewing. After thirty minutes or so, he was escorted from the building by security.

I would like to say that this man and his son healed their relationship, but that was not the case. The father had a heart attack during the middle of one of his tirades, and dropped dead on the spot. He was in his early thirties. Misplaced anger is not only bad for our relationships; it is terrible on our physical body.

If you find that your anger is uncontrollable, there may be deeper issues. Perhaps you grew up with an angry parent and raging was modeled as a way to handle

145

conflict. If so, contact a church pastor or Christian counselor who can help you heal from the damage that anger has caused in your own life. Be the one to stop the cycle of destructive rage in your family.

We must also be aware of the unspoken messages we send when talking with our teen. Facial expression, posture and tone of voice speak volumes during a discussion. If our teen senses a lack of concern or judgment based on outward appearance, they will be less likely to communicate their deepest thoughts and feelings. One easy way for recognizing our nasty looks or lack of volume control is to ask our spouse or those closest to us if they see these as a concern. It is likely that we behave similarly when having discussions with them. Accountability in this area has the potential to greatly improve communication with our teen and with others.

There are several more elements we must include if we desire positive communication with our teens. First, we must be sure to keep our attitudes in check in the same way we expect our teens to check theirs. Ditch attitudes like "I'm too busy for you right now." When teens feel their thoughts are unimportant, they will find someone to talk with, but it won't be us if we continue to disregard them. We must also lay aside the "know it all" attitude. Have you ever assumed you knew what your teen was going to say, only to shut them down before they were finished? Be sure to give them the opportunity to complete their thoughts, even if you find you were right. Abstain from using the silent treatment or sarcasm to express disapproval to your teen. Both the silent treatment and sarcasm show teens that we are more interested in "winning" than resolving the issue. A power struggle often ensues, and neither party wins. Be sure to avoid bringing up past events and only discuss the issue at hand. This will keep the layers of resentment from building and you are more likely to resolve the issue at hand. Be sure to use "I" statements when making points during a disagreement. Avoid phrases like, "You make me so mad" and replace those words with, "I feel angry when _____." "I" statements keep the focus on how you feel and keep your teen off the defensive. Finally, we must be sure to avoid interrupting our teen when they are making a point during an argument. Remember, they know our "buttons" as well as we know theirs and there may be times they push them. Once again, WE are the adults. We must remain calm, or walk away until we can do so. If we choose to engage in a power struggle, we lose.

We must remember to give our teen undivided attention when they talk with us. We need to stop what we are doing, look them in the eye, and show genuine interest in the conversation. If the timing is bad, we can assure our teen that we want to hear what they have to say, and then agree on a time that we can meet to finish the discussion. If television, phone calls or the computer become more important than your teen on a continual basis, I challenge you to re-evaluate your priorities.

Listening is also a crucial skill we must acquire in order to effectively communicate with our teens. As we actively listen, our teens feel supported, understood and their self-esteem increases. By reflectively listening, we verify what our teens are saying and let them know we hear each word they speak. Teens require a LOT of active and reflective listening!

Practice good listening with your teen by using some of the following:

➢ "So, what I hear you saying is _____." Repeat to your teen what you hear them saying. You may be surprised to find that what you heard is completely different from what they said.

➢ "So, you feel I am being unfair when I make you clean your room." (Teens will either say "yes" or elaborate on their feelings…continue reflective listening by simply repeating what they are saying.)

➢ "I'm not sure I understand what you are saying. Can you give me an example?"

➢ "Can you help me understand your reason for saying (or doing) _____?"

By implementing these phrases, teens realize it is safe to have open communication with us. Most importantly, our teen will feel that we are listening with our heart. Proverbs 23:7 reminds us, "As a man thinks in his heart, so is he." Our teens will know who we really are by the behavior we exhibit and the words we communicate.

Keeping our teen's confidences is also a crucial part of positive communication. Nothing is more embarrassing to a teen than for a parent to list all of his/her shortcomings in front of friends. I have seen this happen more than once. Without thinking, parents say things like, "He is so scared to try out for football and I just don't know why." When broadcasting our teen's shortcomings or confidences to others, we drive a deep wedge in the heart of the relationship. If your teen tells you something in confidence, keep the confidence. Let your teen know that, other than your spouse, their secret is safe with you and then abide by your word. By keeping confidences, trust is developed and a bond of mutual respect is formed. If you violate your teen's confidence, quickly make amends. It may take time, but by proving you are trustworthy, the relationship can be healed in this area.

When talking with your teen, remind them that nothing can remove your love for them. The Bible calls this "agape" or unconditional love and it is a powerful builder of self-esteem in teens. With that said, we must also remind our teens that we are accountable to God for how we raise them. Proverbs 22:6 says, "Train up a child in the way he should go and when he is old, he will not depart from it." As long as our teens are at home, we are accountable to them and most importantly, to God, for teaching them the TRUTH in love. Remember to speak with tongues of love. If your daughter comes downstairs to go out and looks inappropriate, let her know the truth, in

149

love. For example, "Honey, I can appreciate that you like what you have on, but it is not appropriate. Please go back and change if you would like to leave the house." Do not argue the "You're so unfair" statement. Continue making your point. "Honey, we have discussed what is appropriate for you to wear out of our home. If you would like to go out, please go change your clothes." They will eventually realize the time they could be spending with

Decline the opportunity to get caught up in issues that don't have long term moral or ethical significance.

friends is wasting, and they will change their clothes. If you fear your teen will change clothes once they leave home, refer to Chapter 2. Most importantly, remember to pick your battles. Decline the opportunity to get caught up in issues that don't have long term moral or ethical significance.

The most important step of communication with our teen is to always speak the TRUTH. Not OUR truth, but THE TRUTH of God's Word. For example, you come home one night and your teen is watching a rated "R" movie. You remind them they should not be watching it and they respond, "Come on dad, I see worse than this at school." Lovingly remind them that while they may see worse at school, God's Word has a lot to say about what they are watching. Find scripture to address the concerns you have with your teen, and tell them the truth, in love. For example, you may say something like, "Honey, I know you see things at school that are really inappropriate, but I know that you really value what God's Word says too." Then, share a scripture with them which pertains to that particular issue. "But what if my teen doesn't respond positively when I share God's Word with them?" Do it anyway. When the Bible says, "The truth will set them free," it means just what it says. Remember, the key is to share it in love. If we preach, or try to cram it down their proverbial throats, it WILL backfire on us. Just keep sharing the truth, in love. God will honor your efforts. If they argue with you, remind them in a most kind way, "Honey, I didn't write these words, God did. I'm just sharing what He has to say with you." Then, pray that your teen will hear the truth and respond with a repentant heart.

Mutual respect is also a must in the parent-teen relationship. While we are responsible for how we treat our teen, we are responsible for how we allow our teen to treat us. When teens show disrespect, there are some appropriate responses and consequences that we must put into place. Remember, parents who fail to correct disrespect out of fear of pushing their child away are open to great heartache in the future. The moment disrespect begins, address it.

We must first define disrespect. Disrespect is most often present when a person shows no concern for another's time, feelings or existence. A teenager yelling, "I'm sick of you telling me what to do" when given a chore is obvious disrespect, but what about those smaller actions that we often overlook? When you ask your teen to get off of the phone and ten minutes later they are still talking, is that disrespect? Perhaps, or maybe it is just your teen being selfish. So how do we evaluate what disrespect is and how do we address it?

Through my counseling experience, I have found that the definition of disrespect often differs from home to home. Therefore, you as the parent will have to decide when you feel disrespected…and you will know. It appears that there is an "inborn detector" for disrespect, and it beeps loudly once we have been disrespected. Keep in mind that if your teen's actions show no concern for your time, feelings or existence, you are being disrespected.

Once you feel disrespected, following these steps from LiveStrong.com may help you address the situation:

1. Respond instead of react. If you are too angry to respond, leave the room and let your teen know when you will be back to address the issue.

2. Be simple and specific when telling your teen how their behavior was disrespectful. Example: "I felt disrespected when I asked you to hang up the phone and you chose to continue talking."

3. Allow your teen to speak. What they say has merit and you may find they were not intending to be disrespectful at all.

4. Avoid name–calling and showing resentment. When we use name–calling, we model that this is appropriate behavior for our kids.

5. Stay focused. If your teen tries to derail you or get you upset, continue repeating the issue at hand and let them know you will not be distracted.

6. Invite your teen's solution to the problem once the issue has been addressed.

7. Let it go after the issue is resolved. If a consequence is necessary, give one that "fits the crime." Never issue consequences when angry. We usually go overboard and if we go back on our word, our teens may not believe us the next time consequences are issued. (Miller, "How to Deal")

The previous suggestions work well for teens who are responsive, but what about those tougher teens who have an attitude of indifference? Teens who regularly argue, pose a threat, or refuse to abide by your rules may require more structured discipline. For some teens, consequences mean little, and if they do care, they certainly won't let us know. For example, I have a friend whose son was involved in pornography. She went as far as removing everything from his life, including the door on his room so he had no privacy. His response was always, "I don't care." These teens are tough, and we must have tougher tools in order to respond effectively. The following are additional suggestions from LiveStrong.com:

1. Set up a Behavior Contract with your teen. If your teen consistently seems to "forget" or misinterpret the rules of home, you can clarify your intentions by writing a contract with him/her. Involving your teen when making the rules may lead to greater success of follow-through. Your teen may also be more encouraged to comply if you promise specific rewards in the contract. Make the rules as simple and clear as possible to avoid

causing your teen to feel bullied or overwhelmed. For example, write, "_____ will be home by 10 p.m. every night," rather than, "_____ will come home as soon as he is asked to come home." Discuss the rules with your teen so they are fully understood, then sign the contract, along with your teen, and post it in a visible location.

2. Have a check-in routine for your teen. Agree in your home behavior contract that your teen must give you concrete information about his/her plans (e.g. the address of the party or her friend's mother's phone number). If details are not provided, your teen will not be permitted to leave the house.

3. Be consistent! According to the American Academy of Pediatrics, parents who don't follow through with punishments reinforce misbehavior because inconsistency confuses teens and can cause them to disrespect parental authority. Alternately, consistency teaches teens that they can't bend rules as they see fit. The good news is that you can establish consistency from this point forward and your teen will eventually realize that you are serious. (Miller, "Tips")

Remember parents, there are limits to consequences. Experience shows that the most effective consequences only last a few hours for minor violations and a few days for more serious ones. If you find that your consequences are not being taken seriously, the next step is to get outside help. A Godly, well-trained counselor in the area of teen issues can be very helpful. Depending on the severity of the behavior, counseling for the entire family may be needed.

A lack of self-esteem is often at the base of our teen's behaviors. Fortunately, there are things we can do as parents to help build our teen's self-esteem. The first thing you can do is simply ask your teen how you can pray for them each day. While this may be foreign to your teen in the formative years, it will be something they often treasure when they are older. James 5:16 (KJV) reminds us that "the prayers of a righteous man [woman] availeth much." God has given us the authority and power to pray for our kids! Never underestimate the power your prayers have over your teen's

The first thing you can do is simply ask your teen how you can pray for them each day.

life. If you are not praying for your child on a daily basis, make today the beginning. If your teen says they don't need prayer, pray for them anyway. God delights in answering the prayers of parents for their children (Matthew 7:7-11). Keep a journal of prayers for your children. You may even wish to share that journal someday. It will be a powerful reminder of your love for them.

If you experience a period where your teen doubts their faith and all they have been taught growing up, don't fret. Teens often come to a "crisis of faith" where they ask, "Do I believe this because it's what Mom and Dad believe, or is it true in my own life?" During these times, guide your teen. Instead of saying, "How could you doubt God after all we have taught you?" ask, "What are your questions?" Be willing to listen and gently guide them while they ponder their doubts. Remember, we are responsible for teaching TRUTH and we can do so in love as we walk alongside them. If we don't, the culture is waiting and willing to teach them for us. Be proactive and assertive in including the Word of God in all you do with your teen. If you are unsure of scripture that applies to your circumstance at the time, the internet can be your best friend. Type these words in your search engine, "Bible verse confrontation" or whatever the issue might be. It's all in God's Word, and the TRUTH always enhances self-esteem.

Spending quality time with your teen is also a way to boost self-esteem. While teens often long to spend time with their friends, time with family is still important. Make a "date night" with your teen once a week. This night is reserved for the two of you. Allow your teen to help choose what you will do and spend time doing things that are fun. Avoid demanding conversation. Remember, confrontation is not what teens enjoy. Save those "dates" for times when difficult issues must be addressed. "Date night" doesn't have to cost money. Go for a bike ride, hang out at the park, go window shopping or play a game on the computer. Family events are important as well. Teens feel empowered when their family is solid. Whether a single-parent home or one where both parents are present, let your teen know that the family structure is built on God's foundation and that family time will be priority. Create stability for you and your teen by scheduling a recurring day and time for family outings.

The greatest self-esteem we can give our teen is grounded in their identity in Christ. This is not a one day lesson, it is a life-long lesson. Our teens must know who Christ says they are so they have a way to combat the lies culture feeds them. Knowing who they are in Christ can also prevent meltdowns. For example, I take Cindy to buy a new pair of shoes at the store. Cindy is elated...until the following day. The next morning, she hates the shoes and is not wearing them. I say, "Guess what, I paid more for those shoes than I did for my car and you are GOING TO wear them. I don't care if you don't like them." Cindy may wear the shoes, but I have just dismissed her from my life in this discussion. She will go to others to talk about those shoes, but she will never do so with me. When our kid's identity in Christ is solid, He will determine their value, not the shoes they are wearing.

So how do we teach our teens the TRUTH of their identity in Christ? The following are some suggestions:

➢ Remind your teen that God gave them unique personalities, talents and gifts especially designed for them.

➢ Verbally applaud your teen for their WHO instead of their DO. Their identity must be in WHO they are in Christ, otherwise, when they fail, they will believe they are worthless. While it is ok to tell them they did something well, focus the majority of praise on their wonderful qualities which contributed to their great performance.

➤ Solicit your teen's opinion. This allows your teen to know that you have confidence in what they think. Teens often enjoy being treated like an adult.

➤ Encourage the use of their gifts and talents. Teens want to have value in society. When teens use their talents outside of our home, they often receive acceptance. When I judged a large teen talent show, I saw this first-hand. One of the shy boys in the school performed an amazing act. Afterward, everyone congratulated him and he gained recognition and friends he had never experienced. In turn, his self-esteem grew and he was willing to take more chances.

➤ Discourage your teen from comparing themselves with others. Help keep your teen focused on their goals and dreams so there is not time to worry about what others are doing.

➤ Reinforce friendships that are positive. For more information on friendships, visit Chapter 6.

➤ Stay engaged with your teen. Parents often feel they have little influence over their lives and that teens are not listening. Remain engaged or culture will become their truth.

With prayer, love and the TRUTH of God's Word, we can conquer the lies of culture and raise confident teens. God's Word reminds us that we "are in this world but not of the world" when we are followers of Christ (John 15:19). We may not escape the cultural challenges that surround us, but we can confront them head on with confidence when we parent our teens God's way.

PARENT PAUSE:

1. What are some patterns of communication that need to improve between you and your teen? What will you do to improve them?

2. When you feel disrespected, what are some healthy ways you will choose to handle such disrespect?

3. Have you asked your teen how you can pray for them today?

CHAPTER ELEVEN

THE TOUGH QUESTIONS

"And let us not grow weary of doing good, for in due season we will reap, if we do not give up."

-Galatians 6:9

While writing this book, I asked for parent input. I was overwhelmed with the number of concerns that were sent my way. As a result, I created this Question and Answer section.

My prayer is that those of you facing the "tougher topics" will find wisdom, hope and TRUTH in the answers provided. Most come from experience as I counseled parents facing difficult times. A few come from watching parents with great wisdom do "whatever it takes" to give their teen what they need to succeed in life. These questions are real concerns sent from real parents just like you. Remember, you are never alone in this role. Others have walked these paths, and most importantly, God knows how to get you and your teen where He desires for you to be.

Q: How can I raise my teen to be Godly when my spouse is not a Christian and does not support Godly principles of parenting?

A: When co-parenting with a spouse who is not a Christian, we are in some ways acting as a single parent. While our unsaved spouse loves our teen, they are incapable of supporting or demonstrating Godly principles because they do not have a relationship with Christ. If your unsaved spouse is male, find a Godly man that your teen can connect with on a healthy level. Godly grandfathers, uncles or church leaders can be great examples of how a Godly man interacts with others and responds to life's challenges. If your unsaved spouse is female, do the same for your teen by choosing a Godly woman. Godly grandmothers, aunts or teachers can be powerful examples of God's love and leadership. As the parent who knows Christ, we must also be sure that we demonstrate love to our spouse without compromising our beliefs. If our unsaved spouse asks us to do something that goes against God's Word, we must always follow God's Word. Be sure your teen knows that while you love your spouse, your commitment to Christ is first because that is what God's word commands. As love always leads when this occurs, maintain firm boundaries. This allows our teen to learn the discipline of setting firm boundaries in their own life. Finally, pray with your teen. Model a healthy prayer life and read God's Word with your teen so that TRUTH is planted in their hearts. When you do so, your teen will be capable of making better decisions from God's Word when your spouse allows or encourages ungodly behavior. If your teen is unsaved, pray for their salvation and continue modeling the example of Christ in your home. Please remember, the Holy Spirit is what draws people's hearts to know Christ. While you can be a Godly influence to your spouse and children, prayer really is most important, and ultimately, it is their choice to believe. God will do whatever he needs to do to draw your spouse and teen to Himself. We must pray and then stay out of the way. Once we move, the Holy Spirit has the opportunity to do things that we are incapable of doing on a human level. God's will is that "all come to repentance," and that certainly includes everyone in your family.

Q: How do I balance my role as a parent and all my other requirements without losing my patience or losing my mind?

A: The first thing to realize is that you may not get it all done, and THAT'S OK. Priorities include purpose. Begin each day by asking God what His purpose is for you on THAT DAY, then listen to his response. Some days will be busier than others, but we must get rid of things that waste time EVERY day. First, limit your time on social media. Give yourself 30 minutes to "like" things on Facebook or surf Pinterest. When 30 minutes is up, time is up for the day. Secondly, make a "to-do" list. Goals are often accomplished once they are written down. When goals are written down, they keep us focused, and we are able to choose between pressing and not-so-pressing items we must do for the day. For example, you may "want" to clean the garage, but guests are coming in from out of town. Prioritize, and worry about areas that are highly visible and will be most visited. The garage will still be there when your guests leave. Next, stop worrying. The Bible reminds us that worrying does not add one second to our life – it can actually WASTE many hours! When we worry, we are distracted. As a result, we are more lethargic and begin to spiral downward when giving in to our feelings of worry. Begin your mornings with a quiet time. Give your concerns to God, trust Him by putting it in His hands and get busy with your "to-do" list. If you do not finish your list for the day, move the incomplete items to the next day. There are only 24 hours in a day, and let's face it, some days just don't go the way we planned. It's OK! If your teen or anyone else is upset because you are not "super-mom" or "super-dad," remind them that you could always use their help, that you are human, and that you have done your best for the day. Our teens appreciate us most when we are honest with them. Remain calm as you talk with your teen. Raving parents do not make for effective parents and we sacrifice respect in our teen's eyes when we "lose it." If you lose your cool, quickly ask your teen to forgive you, then, retreat and take a "parent time out." It is also healthy to schedule some "me" time. If getting a manicure or taking a bath relaxes you, take an hour for you when you are feeling stressed out. This will help you recharge your battery in order to be the healthy parent your teen needs.

Q: How can I motivate a teen who has no ambition?

A: There are two forms of motivation: love and fear. Before applying either, we must rule out other factors which can lead to a lack of motivation in teens. Depression, ADD, ADHD and ODD (Oppositional Defiant Disorder) are just some of the factors that can inhibit motivation in our teens. Have your teen evaluated by a physician if physical concerns are present. If physical concerns are not interfering with motivation, there are steps to take. First, find something to appreciate. It may be difficult, but find something to compliment in your teen, even if it's how nicely they took out the trash or their good sense of humor. I love the line from the movie *Steel Magnolias* when Dolly Parton's character says about her daughter's shady boyfriend, "The nicest thing I can say about him is all his tattoos are spelled right." (*Steel Magnolias*) Everyone likes to be complimented and we can always find something to appreciate. Secondly, use humor, not sarcasm, when approaching your teen about a subject. While the situation may be anything but funny, find some way to address the issue with some humor. For example, "You're going to have to drop me off at the nursing home on your bike when you're 50 if you don't take that driver's test." Third, issue trade-offs. If your teen would like for you to do something for him/her, let them know you expect something in return. For example, your teen wants to go to the movies with friends, but you want the closet you asked them to clean a week ago to be completely clean before they can leave. Be sure you reinforce your boundaries. Allow your teen to feel the effects of their "unmotivated choices" if they don't comply. If your teen chooses not to study during the school year, they will be forced to attend summer school. While it is hard to watch our teens fail, it is often what teens need. Failure can be a great motivator because teens fear having to repeat the same consequence. After your teen faces natural consequences for their decisions, ask them questions such as, "What did you learn from this and what can you do better next time?" For those tougher teens who have no need for progress, evaluation is a must. As mentioned earlier, medical issues often interfere with motivation and once your teen is treated by a professional, many interests will return.

Q: What if my child chooses a bi-sexual or homo-sexual relationship?

A: One issue severely attacking our teen's self-esteem today includes sexual identity. While culture pushes our "choice to decide," the Bible presents the

TRUTH. When teens struggle with their sexual identity, they have begun to believe the lies of modern culture. What does the TRUTH of God's Word say? Mark 10:6-9 reminds us, "At the beginning of creation God made them male and female. For this reason a man will leave his father and mother and be united to his wife, and the two will become one flesh. So they are no longer two, but one. Therefore what God has joined together, let man not separate." The word "wife" in Hebrew and Greek always means woman. Never does it refer to the submissive role of a male partner and nowhere in scripture does God abdicate or allow same sex relationships. He calls it sin. Reminding our teen of the consequences that same sex sin can bring is crucial, but we must do so in love. Jesus taught that all people are equally loved and forgiven in the eyes of God – but He never condoned sin of any sort. Instead, He calls us to leave our life of sin if we want to genuinely follow Him. If God had intended to condone same sex relationships, He would have never given the commandment in Genesis 9:7, "Be fruitful and increase in number, multiply on the earth and increase upon it." Two men or two women cannot procreate. God speaks truth in love, but He never goes back on His Word, no matter what culture or opinions the media may offer. His truth will not change according to I Peter 1:25.

If your teen is determined to live a bisexual or homo-sexual lifestyle, remind them that nothing they do can remove the love you have for them. Ask your teen what they need from you, and how you can help. Be honest about your feelings, but remember that lectures, questions or quoting scripture will probably not be helpful as an initial part of the discussion. When the opportunity is right to ask those tougher questions, be ready to hear the tough answers. Some answers may hurt, but remember, their answers are based on their perspective and mindset. The more open communication you have, the better your conversations will be with your teen about his/her "new identity." While it is important to be honest with one another, choose your words carefully. Pose your questions as if you are trying to understand their choice. I have seen parents say very unproductive things such as, "I wish you would just snap out of this phase. Trisha is so cute. Why can't you just go out with her and stop being gay?" This is not helpful and will force your teen in the opposite direction. This is going to be a journey and possibly a long one. Your teen needs your guidance and the TRUTH of God's Word spoken in love more than they need to hear how wrong they are. At some level, they know.

In ministering to and counseling those with same sex attraction, the one thing I have been told repeatedly is the importance of being loved. Those involved in homosexual relationships have often said, "If those talking to me during my teen years had shown me, in love, what the Bible said about same sex attraction instead of turning their back on me, I don't think I would be where I am today." Fortunately, I have seen the power of love, combined with God's Word, deliver men and women from very deep involvement in the homosexual lifestyle. It is a beautiful thing to watch God's love and TRUTH transform others.

As you feel and experience things through this journey as a parent, talk with a wise and Godly friend, pastor or counselor. Journal your thoughts, but be particular about what thoughts you share with your teen. Everything you are feeling about their decision does not need to be shared. God knows your heart is breaking and He is able to bring you peace even through this difficult time. As a word of caution, do not be disappointed if your teen refuses counseling for this issue. They see nothing wrong with their choice because they are deceived, so most likely they will refuse to go on their own. Instead, find a mentor of the same sex that can be in their life to help them grow spiritually. Change is what you are wanting. Exposing them to scriptural truths through mentors who live God's Word, and do so in love, is a daily reminder of TRUTH staring them in the face. Typically, there are deeper issues than homosexuality at the root, and family counseling may be a good option so those roots can be exposed and the teen does not feel that they are being singled out.

Remember, the Holy Spirit knows how to transform with grace and truth. He will give you peace and will never give up on you or your child. His will is that "everyone come to repentance" (2 Peter 3:9). He loves you and your teen so very much.

Q: What do I do when my teen rejects God and wants nothing to do with the church?

A: First of all, be assured that you are not the first parent to have your teen turn away from his/her faith or the Godly values you have instilled in them. The story of the Prodigal son in Luke 15 is a firm reminder that even the best of parents can have children who choose their own way. If your teen has decided to turn against the Christian values you have raised them to believe, there are some things you must do to help guide them back "home." First, continue to show them Christ – not in a pushover, "religious" kind of way, but through your lifestyle. Teens that turn from Christ are not seeing or understanding the TRUTH of who He really is. As I have stressed throughout the book, our job as parents is to teach them the TRUTH. We must also take the posture God takes with us. How many times have we turned away to do our own thing, with no consideration for His ways? While we can focus on our teens, we are no different in some respects. Just as God never turns His back on us, we must keep our arms extended to our teen and let them know we will welcome them home. Is it easy to wait? No. Is it necessary? Yes. During the waiting, find opportune times to listen to your teen as to why they refuse Christ. When you have an open conversation with your teen you will know how to pray more specifically. The most important guide we have is the example of what our Heavenly Father does when we "turn our back" on Him. First, He continues to reach out to us. Secondly, He teaches us the TRUTH in love through His Word. Remember when He met the Samaritan woman at the well? He didn't yell, "What is wrong with you?" He simply spoke the truth about her husbands, and then shared "living water" (John 4:10). Third, remind your teen that God is bigger than "feelings." Teens are very "feeling" oriented, and they often base what they are "feeling" on how God is working in their life. Last, God sends others to minister to us when we have walked away from Him. Allow others to minister to your teen by insisting they attend church. While it may be something they don't like, church provides an opportunity for God to speak to their heart when they are surrounded by those who know Christ. Most importantly, remember that your teen is learning through the "unspoken sermon" you are living out in front of them daily. As you pray for your teen, ask God to help you be a Godly parent.

Q: My spouse and I are Christians, but we do not agree on disciplinary actions for our teen. What can we do?

A: It does not take long for teens to figure out that lack of unity between parents in the area of discipline can work in their favor. After all, if they don't get the answer they want from one parent, they just go to the other. The key to disciplining is always a unified front. If you disagree about discipline, never do it in front of your teen. This creates a troubling environment for teens as well as your marriage, and only generates more chaos. Talk about your disagreements regarding discipline at a time when you and your spouse can do so calmly. Since you are both Christians, base your disciplining decisions on God's Word. If your spouse, for example, allows your teen daughter to wear clothes that do not edify Christ, refer him/her to Chapter 2 of this book on dress and study the scriptures used there. During your discussion, decide what values matter most to you as parents. Be sure to recognize your partner's positive parenting skills. Focusing on their weaknesses is not healthy. Talk with one another about your parenting strengths and discuss who will be the better parent to make decisions in various areas. You must also discuss openly why you each want to parent the way you do. Sometimes we simply parent the same way we were raised instead of considering that those methods may not have been healthy. The most controversial part of disciplining usually comes from "how" teens are disciplined. If your spouse tends to be sterner with discipline, talk with them to find the reasoning behind their decision. Most importantly, pray together as a couple and ask God to give you clear direction in the area of discipline.

Q: My teen has threatened suicide on more than one occasion. What can I do to help?

A: First of all, take every threat of suicide that your teen mentions seriously. Communication is key when talking with a suicidal teen. Talk with your teen about their feelings and thank them for being willing to talk openly with you. Be sure you recognize the warning signs of suicide. Signs that a teen may be seriously contemplating suicide are:

- An oral comment or written note indicating a desire to die

- Previous suicidal attempts

- Statements of hopelessness

- Art or notes that convey thoughts of death

- Increased absenteeism from school

- Unexplained decline in academic performance

- Self-inflicted injuries

- Giving away favorite possessions to family or friends

- Social withdrawal

- Dramatic personality changes

- Unusual neglect of physical appearance

Once your teen threatens suicide, do not let them out of your sight until you feel they are safe. It only takes moments for them to make a life-changing move. If they are serious, they will appreciate your concern.

Teens generally want to be talked out of ending their lives and want to know you care. Once a threat has been made, immediately contact someone who can help you. During the day, make an emergency appointment with your physician. When a threat is made after office hours, contact authorities to help you get your teen the help they need. Let your teen know that you will go to every extreme necessary to preserve their life. If you are at work or away from home when the threat is made, contact someone immediately who can go and be with your teen. DO NOT LEAVE YOUR TEEN ALONE. If no one is available, call police and have them go to your home until you arrive. There is medical help and counseling available. Be sure to get you and your teen the help that is needed to preserve the life of the one you so dearly love.

Holly is a mom who has experienced the death of a teen through suicide and gives powerful advice in Appendix A.

Q: My teen performs self-injurious acts on herself, including cutting herself with razors. What can I do to help her?

A: Self-harm is a way of expressing and dealing with deep distress and emotional pain. As counterintuitive as it may sound to those on the outside, those who participate in self-injury do so because it makes them feel better and they often feel they have no choice. It is usually the best way they know to cope with feelings of sadness, self-loathing, emptiness, guilt, and rage. Although they feel good for a while, the relief that comes as a result of self-injury doesn't last, and the process is repeated. Most who self-injure do so in secret. The guilt and secrecy affect relationships with others and they often feel very alone, therefore sending them into a downward spiral to more self-injury. Contrary to popular belief, self-injurers do not want to die. They want to end their pain. Unfortunately, some end their lives mistakenly. Although their scars may be small, never assume their pain is small. The seriousness of the injury is in no way reflective of the amount of pain they are feeling. Fortunately, there are effective ways to deal with self-injury. First, make sure your teen has at least two people available that they trust and can call when they feel they are going to self-harm. Accountability is their life-line. When a "cutter" knows they have someone to talk with before they injure themselves, they will often call versus cutting. You must also have your teen create a list of ten things they can do if they feel like "cutting." Have your teen wear a rubber band on their arm and when they feel like "cutting," have them pop themselves, repeatedly if necessary, to release pain. They may also choose to draw red on their skin with a marker in the place where they want to cut. Drawing or scribbling on paper with ink or red paint is also helpful. Have them release their feelings in a journal, or write all of their frustration, hurt and anger on a piece of paper and rip it up. If your teen cuts for a calming effect, have them wrap up in a warm blanket or cuddle with an animal. If they cut because they feel disconnected or numb, have them hold a cold ice-cube in the crook of their leg, take a cold shower, or eat something with a very strong taste like a jalapeno or chili peppers. While these are only temporary fixes, you must find the root of the problem. Involve your teen with a counselor who understands self-injury and, if possible, who is a former victim themselves. Families of those who self-injure will also benefit from counseling. Pray for your teen, and ask God to heal the hurt and pain they are experiencing. Show unconditional love for your teen and never shame them for cutting – it will only lead to more misbehavior. Highlight the positive things they do and provide a safe physical environment by asking them to give you all of their self-injurious materials. A "cutter" uses everything from razor blades to erasers. You can be a part of keeping them safe by insisting they attend counseling and if necessary, hospitalization with trained physicians until the issue is resolved.

Q: I am a single parent and I struggle with raising a teen on my own. What are some of the most important things I need to do as a single parent to raise her the way God intends?

A: While being a single parent is never easy, God promises that He will be a "husband to the husbandless" and a "father to the fatherless." He will provide the help you need to raise a successful teen. One way He provides is through friends. Friends can help lighten the load of being a single parent in several ways. They may take your teen to practice when you have to work or help your teen with homework. They may also stay with your teen when you have to be gone. These are just a few examples of how friends can assist you. They can also aid in having a life outside your parenting role. While your parenting role is important, it is also important that you make time for "you."

It is crucial that your teen knows you are the only adult in the home. Sometimes teens try to compensate and play the role of adult when one parent is missing. Assure the teen that you are the parent by finding others to confide in. Keeping the role of parent/friend balance is important. Single parents often make their teen their confidant. While it is good to share information, it is important to provide your teen with the security that you are the parent. Inquire about help for single parents at your church. If it is not provided, begin a single parent group or strongly suggest that your church organize one. There are many single parents, and a community of believers supporting one another is important. Remember, boundaries create safety for teens. Stability is also an important factor in maintaining your home. Assure your teen that there are some expectations/boundaries that will not change. Some of those are standard bed times, curfews and homework checks. Don't be afraid to set expectations/boundaries and follow through. Never be afraid to solicit help from people you trust.

Q: My child was molested by our babysitter when she was young. We found out when she began acting out in ways we didn't understand. What advice would you give to parents whose child has been raped or molested?

A: Childhood and adolescent sexual abuse damages the mind, body and spirit of a human being. To understand sexual abuse, we must first know some secondary symptoms that abuse survivors experience. Sexual abuse survivors often display the following behaviors:

- Anger management problems
- Loneliness/isolation
- Anxiety and fear
- Sleep disorders
- Trust issues
- Low self-image
- Disconnection from self, others and God
- Substance abuse
- Intimacy issues
- Depression
- Stress-related physical problems
- Self-mutilation

- Body image problems and eating disorders
- Dysfunctional relationships
- Difficulty concentrating
- Basing their self-value on performance
- Spiritual detachment or disengagement

Once sexual abuse has been revealed, there are crucial steps parents must take to protect teens. First, believe them until proven otherwise. Next, tell your teen how proud you are of them for coming to you and for telling you. Let them know that you will do whatever it takes to keep them safe, and never insist that your teen have any contact with their abuser. Be sure to report the abuse to the authorities. Most perpetrators have more than one victim. Reporting the abuser will not only help keep your child safe, but will protect other victims or potential victims. Remember, abusers often tell victims they will hurt them or someone else if they are reported. It is crucial that we remind our teen that we will keep them safe and that we will disclose to authorities if the abuser threatens to harm anyone else. We must also keep in mind that most abusers are family members or someone close to the child; therefore, reporting a perpetrator may be difficult. Regardless, report them – this is your child's life at stake. Never assume that your child's lack of emotion about the event indicates a lack of abuse. Victims often harbor such pain that they have become numb and unable to express feelings. Allow your teen to work on their issues as a result of the abuse in

SHANNON PERRY

professional counseling. Be sure they have access to private sessions with their counselor. Teens often find it difficult to talk about such painful occurrences in front of others, especially family members. We must also be sensitive to "triggers." Triggers are things that can cause our teen to remember the abuse. Even certain smells may trigger the emotions as a result of abuse. Allow your teen to tell you whatever they are feeling. One of the worst side effects of abuse is shame. Allow your teen to correspond with other survivors in a Christian-based, controlled group and talk about the ways God is healing them from their experience. As a parent, you must also forgive yourself. Perpetrators are cunning and they find opportune times to prey on their victims when authority figures are not around.

Finally, remember that God "will repay you for the years the locusts have eaten" (Joel 2:25). God is able to restore health and wholeness to your teen after the experience of abuse.

Q: What do I do if I find out my teen is sexually active? What if they become pregnant?

A: While it is important to address your teen's sexual activity, it is also important to keep the doors of communication open and maintain your relationship with your teen. You must confront your teen's behavior openly and honestly.

First of all, remind your teen that they are precious in God's eyes and in yours. Next, introduce the subject of his/her sexual behavior in a non-threatening way. For example, you may say something like, "I was standing by your door the other day and overheard you discussing a recent encounter with your girl-friend/boyfriend." Allow your teen to explain the situation and listen. After they admit their sexual encounter, it is appropriate to discuss the consequences of their actions. Requiring that your teen terminate the relationship with their boyfriend/girlfriend is not out of the question. It is also important to talk with the parents of the boyfriend/girlfriend about the sexual encounter. If the other set of parents do not see a problem, you must set firm ground rules. If your teen continues to see the boyfriend/girlfriend, it will only be on supervised dates, and those dates may not be at the home or on an outing with the other parents.

If our teen becomes pregnant, there are several things we must do as parents. First, remember that life is precious, both your teen's life as well as the baby's. Remember that fear will come and play a large part in the decisions that are made. Fear of the future, fear of not finishing school and fear of what others will think are only some of the thoughts that your teen will face. As a Christian parent, assure your teen that you will stand by them and that you will pray with them to make the right decision as far as adoption or keeping the baby. Psalm 139:13-16 reminds us that abortion is not an option. Help your teen stand on the TRUTH and pray with them as they work through this difficult time. Get your teen daughter the medical attention she needs immediately upon notification of pregnancy to ensure the baby is healthy. Professional counseling is also encouraged. While you can support your teen in many ways, you cannot make their decisions.

If you are the parents of the baby's father, let the parents of the pregnant teen know that you would like to be kept informed about decisions that are made. Keep the lines of communication as open as possible. Remind your son that he does have responsibility, as he helped create this new life. While he may not make the ultimate decision about adoption, talk with your son about the responsibilities of fatherhood and what will be expected of him in this new role.

APPENDICES

APPENDIX A

HOLLY'S STORY

I had the privilege of meeting Tara and Holly when I was an Elementary School Counselor. I was Tara's counselor throughout her Elementary School years and we spent many special times together. During those years, I watched Tara grow and make many new friends as her self-esteem blossomed. She was a beautiful child and became a precious and loving teenager. She was a shining reflection of her mother, Holly, whose strength and heart is an encouragement to all who know her.

Holly's desire is to share her story so that other children can be saved from the devastating effects of bullying. Her personal and poignant insights are included in this appendix so that parents can intervene in their children's lives before it is too late.

Q: What steps should a parent take when they find out their child is being bullied?

A. "Hug them and tell them you love them and you're going to help them through this problem. Reinforce how much you love them and will always love them.

Relay that bullying is about the other person/people treating your child bad verbally, physically or both. Bullies do negative and mean things to victims because they are suffering physically, mentally or both. Bullies are mean to make themselves feel better and it gives them satisfaction to humiliate good children. Usually bullies are jealous of their victims. My daughter was bullied in Elementary school, Middle School and in High School. Tara did tell adults, including me, on all occasions. She was smart, and jealous people targeted her pure heart and sweet nature."

Q: How can a parent get involved in their child's bullying situation without overstepping their boundaries?

A: "Ask your child the details and where the bullying is occurring. Reinforce your love and support for your child very often. Then ask if your child has told any adults. Make an appointment at the place the incident is happening and speak with the adult in charge. Give specific details of the remarks/assaults. Depending on the adult and actions they take you should remove your child from the situation (school transfer/church, etc.) if you are able. Watch your child closely and ask questions, even if they do not want to talk. Love them and show your love. Pray with them for God's protection and look for signs of behavioral changes. I also monitored her computer use as mean messages were sent via cyber-bullying."

Q: What signs should we look for if our teen is melting down as a result of bullying?

A: "My daughter's sweet personality and happiness changed significantly. She experienced bad moods, crying, not wanting to go to school, not wanting to eat and insisted she sleep with her light on due to fear. Tara regressed and wanted to stay by me and even asked to sleep with me at night. She struggled daily and after school, she was taking out her anger on me. I am safe and we were very close. I sang, prayed, and we did things she enjoyed like baking. Very important, DO NOT LEAVE THEM ALONE. Love them. They are in severe pain and suffering deeply. There is a suicide every 40 seconds and it is the second cause of death in teens statistically."

Q: How can we know when a teen is seriously considering suicide? Are there tell-tale signs?

A: "I NEVER thought my daughter was thinking of this horrible act. I knew she was in severe emotional pain. She started breaking rules, acting out, and yelling at me. She was very stressed out due to the extreme nature of the bullying she was enduring. She would not obey simple rules like eating her dinner. She stopped brushing her teeth and taking her asthma medications. Depression was affecting her logic. I talked to her daily about her activities. However, she did not tell me all of the thoughts in her mind. We can't read their minds. I told her we needed to make an appointment with a counselor if she needed and she said she would go. Tara was funny, told jokes all of the time and loved to visit friends and family. I am proud to say she was the best daughter in the world. God blessed me abundantly. She was my world and my life. Tara was a Girl Scout, taught Vacation Bible School, had high morals and was academically-advanced and recognized for excellence. Her plans were to become a physician to save lives. She was an organ donor at Life Gift and saved eight lives with her precious organs. She was sweet and very loving."

Q: What part should the school system play in the prevention of bullying/suicide?

A: "Have counselors, other parents of their friend's, teachers, every adult in the school watch for signs, listen and enforce the fact that bullying will not be tolerated. Bullying can have negative lifelong consequences – both for the bully and their victims. Bullying in schools is a worldwide problem. This growing epidemic is taking our precious children. The pain of losing your child to suicide is devastating and shocking. The painful loss of your child never goes away. Your child's mind cannot deal with the pain of public humiliation, rumors and harassment that bullying can bring, and the impact of suicidal ideas cannot be underestimated."

Q: What guidance would you give to a parent whose child is threatening suicide?

A: "Tell them how much you and others love them. Reinforce that everyone will be hurting if they do such an act. Monitor them and DO NOT LEAVE THEM ALONE! Help them by calling a Professional Christian Counselor/Psychologist. Admit them if necessary to the hospital. Love is the most needed human emotion. Your child's self-esteem is telling them they are not loved because of the negative comments that have emotionally hurt them. Reinforce how much you, the community, friends and family love and need them to be here. Read with them, do fun things with them, and help them. Your child is breaking inside."

Q: Holly, we know some reading this book have also lost their precious children. What would you say to those parents to help them cope with their loss?

A: "Love is the emotion every human needs to exist happily. Surround yourself with family, friends, church members, pastor, and a good Christian Grief Counselor. My daughter's friends were the most comforting to me. I love my daughter with all of my soul and her friends remind me of her. I still feel horrible for each of them. She never said a word to anyone. Tara left a suicide letter and a detailed explanation. Tara wrote her letter to Jesus. There are many books on this tragic epidemic. Every day is still hard and I pray no one reading this has to deal with this horrible situation. I pray several times daily. My angel is watching over me and all of her many friends, teachers, and family members.

There are several books I would recommend to parents who are grieving and they are listed below:

- ➤ The Bible

- ➤ Heaven is for Real by Todd Burpo

- ➤ 90 Minutes in Heaven by Don Piper

"Shannon, thank you for loving Tara and me. You are loved so much by us."

ANTI-BULLYING HELP

Excerpts from Anti-Bullying Program Written by Shannon Perry and Used by One of the Largest School Systems in the United States
©2013 Shannon Perry/Chae Music

Part 1: Effective Anti-Bullying Guidelines

All schools should have an effective Anti-Bullying policy in place. An effective policy should include and not be limited to the following foundational principles to help ensure your child's safety.

* Clearly define bullying and the various forms of bullying so it is easily understood by both parents AND students.

* Specifically list the consequences for bullying behavior.

* Define and enforce disciplinary action of adults/staff who fail to enforce the bullying policy.

* Designate a staff member as support for parents and students who are victims of bullying.

* Align with the district, state and federal regulations and laws.
* Involve the input of parents, students, staff and district personnel.
* Encourage annual evaluation, revision and updates based on parent, student, staff and district input.
* Publically post the bullying policy on the school's website and the district's website.
* Ensure that the policy is displayed/posted throughout the school, in classrooms and in common areas where students gather.
* Offer and/or require attendance of school-wide lessons that teach appropriate ways to handle a bully.
* Require staff development training regarding bullying prevention/procedures.

The bullying policy should be sent home at the beginning of each school year for all parents AND students to sign. The form should be collected and kept in the child's folder as an agreement to help identify, report, and abstain from any bullying behavior. In addition, the policy should be given to ALL staff members to sign and place in their employment folders as part of their annual contract renewal.

Part 2: "Identifying Bullying Behaviors"
©2013 Shannon Perry/Chae Music

AGGRESSION		
Moderate	**Extreme**	**Life-Threatening**
• Shoving • Tripping • Throwing lightweight objects • Spitting • Hair pulling	• Kicking • Stealing • Damaging property • Isolating to location • Screaming loudly as to damage hearing	• Running over with motorized vehicle • Threatening with gun or weapon • Choking • Head trauma • Physical violence damaging to body

SECLUSION		
Moderate	**Extreme**	**Life-Threatening**
• Seclude others for not using alcohol or drugs • Name calling • Gossiping • Telling secrets • Ignoring	• Framing to take blame • Bribery • Prejudice (wealth, race, religion) • Slandering • Cyberbullying	• Kidnapping • Forced to leave family/friends • Forced drug use • Gang related induction • Human trafficking

VERBAL		
Moderate	**Extreme**	**Life-Threatening**
• Mocking • Cursing • Name calling • Making fun of appearance • Demeaning/degrading character	• Blackmail • Threatening messages by social media • Harassing phone calls • Sexual harassment • Hate mail via postal system	• Death threats • Pre-meditated murder • Verbal threats to property • Pre-meditated endangerment • Verbal threats of destruction to victim/family/friends

APPENDIX C

REFERENCES

"11 Facts about Bullying." *DoSomething.org.* n.d. Web. 17 May 2013. <http://www.dosomething.org/tipsandtools/ 11-facts-about-school-bullying>

"11 Facts about Teens and Drug Abuse." *DoSomething.org.* May 2013. Web. 3 June 2013. <http://www.dosomething.org/tipsandtools/ 11-shocking-facts-about-teens-and-drug-use>

Ahuja, Masuma. "Teens are Spending More Time Consuming Media, on Mobile Devices." *WashingtonPost.com.* 13 Mar 2013. Web. 9 May 2013. <http://articles.washingtonpost.com/2013-03-13/ news/37675597_1_teens-cellphones-video-games>

"Alcohol Abuse Symptoms." *LiveStrong.com.* n.d. Web. 30 May 2013. <http://www.livestrong.com/ alcohol-abuse-symptoms/>

Boyse, Kayla. "Eating Disoders: What Families Need to Know." *Med.Umich.edu.* Oct 2010. Web. 23 Apr 2013. <http://www.med.umich.edu/yourchild/topics/ eatdis.htm>

Brownell, Kelly D. "Eating Disorders: What Causes Eating Disorders?" *Apa.org*. Oct 2011. Web. 24 Apr 2013. <http://www.apa.org/helpcenter/eating.aspx>

"CDC Fact Sheet." *Cdc.gov*. Feb 2013. Web. 7 May 2013. <http://www.cdc.gov/std/stats/ STI-Estimates-Fact-Sheet-Feb-2013.pdf>

"Dating Abuse Statistics." *LoveIsRespect.org*. n.d. Web. 18 June 2013. < http://www.loveisrespect.org/is-this-abuse/dating-violence-statistics>

"Drug Abuse and Addiction: Why Do Some Drug Users Become Addicted, While Others Don't?" *HelpGuide.org*. May 2013. Web. 8 June 2013. <http://www.helpguide.org/mental/ drug_substance_abuse_addiction_signs_effects_treatment.h tm>

"Drug Facts: High School and Youth Trends." *DrugAbuse.gov*. Dec 2012. Web. 1 June 2013. <http://www.drugabuse.gov/publications/drugfacts/ high-school-youth-trends>

"Eating Disorders: Facts About Eating Disorders and the Search for Solutions." *Nimh.Nih.gov*. Pub No. 01-4901. Apr 2013. Web. <http://www.nimh.nih.gov/health/ publications/eating-disorders/complete-index.shtml>

"Facts & Statistics." *MakeBeatsNotBeatdowns.org*. n.d. Web. 17 May 2013. <http://makebeatsnotbeatdowns.org/ facts_new.html>

"Facts About Addition." *Health.HowStuffWorks.com*. n.d. Web. 8 June 2013. <http://health.howstuffworks.com/ mental-health/facts-about-addiction.htm>

Farrel, Pam and Bill. "Sound the Alarm: Teens & Sex." *Crosswalk.com*. 7 May 2013. Web. 12 May 2013. <http://www.crosswalk.com/family/parenting/teens/sound-the-alarm-teens-sex.html>

"Fatality Facts 2011: Teenagers." *Iihs.org*. June 2013. Web. 26 Apr 2013. <http://www.iihs.org/research/fatality.aspx?topicName=Teenagers&year=2011>

Goldburg, Cassie. "National Study: Teen Misuse and Abuse of Prescription Drugs Up 33 Percent Since 2008, Stimulants Contributing to Sustained Rx Epidemic." *DrugFree.org*. 22 April 2013. Web. 31 May 2013. <https://www.drugfree.org/newsroom/pats-2012>

"Hookah Bars." *No-Smoke.org*. n.d. Web. 3 June 2013. <http://www.no-smoke.org/goingsmokefree.php?id=581>

"How Can I Put Parental Controls on My Child's Mobile Phone?" *NetSafe.org*. n.d. Web. 1 June 2013. <http://www.netsafe.org.nz/how-can-i-put-parental-controls-on-my-childs-mobile-phone/>

"How Technology is Influencing Families." *Barna.org*. 23 May 2011. Web. 29 Apr 2013. <http://www.barna.org/family-kids-articles/488-how-technology-is-influencing-families>

"How Teens are Getting Past Parents." *TheTreeNetwork.com*. n.d. Web. 10 May 2013. <https://www.thetreenetwork.com/the-digital-divide-full-study/>

"International Statistics." *DrugFreeWorld.org*. n.d. Web. 1 June 2013. <http://www.drugfreeworld.org/drugfacts/prescription/abuse-international-statistics.html>

LaMance, Ken. "Sexting Laws." *LegalMatch.com*. 6 Jul 2011. Web. 7 May 2013. <http://www.legalmatch.com/ law-library/article/sexting-laws.html>

"Latest Study: 1 in 4 Christian teen girls has an STD - More Christian profanity exposed world-wide!" *Answering-Christianity.com*. n.d. Web. 20 Apr 2013. <http://www.answering-christianity.com/ std_girls_of_christianity.htm>

Lyness, D'Arcy. "Dealing with Bullying: How Does Bullying Make People Feel?" *KidsHealth.org*. Oct 2010. Web. 17 May 2013. <http://kidshealth.org/teen/ your_mind/problems/bullies.html>

"MeetMe - Meet New People: What Parents Need to Know." *CommonSenseMedia.org*. n.d. Web. 1 June 2013. <http://www.commonsensemedia.org/mobile-app-reviews/meetme-meet-new-people>

Miller, Christa. "How to Deal with Disrespectful Children." *LiveStrong.com*. 2 Aug 2010. Web. 5 June 2013. <http://www.livestrong.com/article/ 198665-how-to-deal-with-disrespectful-children/>

Miller, Christa. "Tips for Disciplinig Out of Control Teens." *LiveStrong.com*. 8 May 2010. Web. 5 June 2013. <http://www.livestrong.com/article/ 119049-tips-disciplining-out-control-teens/>

"Modesty Survey." *TheRebelutioncom*. n.d. Web. 2 June 2013. <http://www.therebelution.com/modestysurvey/ browse_190>

"Most Commonly Used OTC Drugs." *Teen-Drug-Abuse.org.*
n.d. Web. 30 May 2013.
<http://www.teen-drug-abuse.org/
teenoverthecounterdrugabuse/commonly-used-otc-
drugs.htm>

"National Reproductive Health Profile: Pregancies, Births
and Abortions." *Guttmacher.org.* May 2013. Web. 4 May
2013. <http://www.guttmacher.org/datacenter/
profiles/US.jsp>

O'Donnell, Jennifer. "A Sample Cell Phone Contract for
Parents and Tweens." *Tweenparenting.About.com.* n.d. Web. 12
May 2013. <http://tweenparenting.about.com/
od/tweenculture/a/Parent-Child-Cell-Phone-
Contracts.htm>

O'Keeffe, Gwenn Schurgin, and Kathleen Clarke-Pearson.
"The Impact of Social Media on Children, Adolescents, and
Families." *Pediatrics.Aappublictions.org.* 28 Mar 2011. Web 12
May 2013. <http://pediatrics.aappublications.org/
content/127/4/800.full>

"OTC Abuse Statistics." *TeenHelp.com.* n.d. Web.
8 June 2013. <http://www.teenhelp.com/
teen-drug-abuse/OTC-abuse-statistics.html>

Rainey, Dennis and Barbara. "Teaching Your Teen About
God's View on Sex." *FamilyLife.com.* n.d. Web. 7 May 2013.
<http://www.familylife.com/articles/topics/parenting/
challenges/sexual-purity/teaching-your-teen-about-gods-
views-on-sex#.Ubx36_lOOdc>

"Reducing Teen STD Risk Requires Focus on Broader Range of Sexual Activities." *Urban.org*. Dec 2000. Web. 21 Apr 2013. <http://www.urban.org/publications/900033.html>

"Sex Education." *FocusontheFamily.com*. 2011. Web. 5 May 2013. <http://www.focusonthefamily.com/socialissues/defending-your-values/sex-education.aspx>

Smith, Catharine. "Serial Sex Offender Admits Using Facebook To Rape And Murder Teen." *HuffingtonPost.com*. 25 May 2011. Web. 10 May 2013. <http://www.huffingtonpost.com/2010/03/08/peter-chapman-admits-usin_n_489674.html>

"Social Media-related Crime Reports Up 780% in Four Years." *Guardian.co.uk*. Dec 2012. Web. 10 May 2013. <http://www.guardian.co.uk/media/2012/dec/27/social-media-crime-facebook-twitter>

Sorvese, Mina. "How to Know if Your Teen is Sexually Active." *HowtodoThings.com*. n.d. Web. 07 May 2013. <http://www.howtodothings.com/family-relationships/how-to-know-if-your-teen-is-sexually-active>

"Statistics." *TeensAgainstAbuse.org*. May 2013. Web. 26 Apr 2013. <http://www.teensagainstabuse.org/index.php?q=statistics>

Steel Magnolias. Dir. Herbert Ross. Perf. Dolly Pardon. TriStar Pictures, 1989. DVD.

Sun, Eryn. "Church Teens not Immune to Sexting." *ChristianPost.com*. 29 Dec 2011. Web. 7 May 2013. <http://www.christianpost.com/news/church-teens-not-immune-to-sexting-66024/>

"Talking about Sex and Puberty: from The Complete Guide to Baby & Child Care." *FocusontheFamily.com*. 1999. Web. 5 May 2013. <http://www.focusonthefamily.com/parenting/schoolage_children/talking-about-sex-and-puberty.aspx>

"Teen Alcohol Abuse Statistics." *TeenHelp.com*. n.d. Web. 8 June 2013. <http://www.teenhelp.com/teen-alcohol-use/teen-alcohol-abuse-statistics.html>

"Teen Health: Overweight Teens." *WebMD.com*. 29 May 2012. Web. 25 Apr 2013. <http://teens.webmd.com/just-for-teens-are-you-overweight>

"Teen Pregnancy Rates by Age Group." *PregnantTeen-Help.org*. Jan 2011. Web. 4 May 2013. <http://www.pregnantteenhelp.org/statistics/teen-pregnancy-rates-by-age-group/>

"Teens & Technology 2013: Summary of Findings." *PewInternet.org*. Nov 2012. Web. 8 May 2013. <http://www.pewinternet.org/Reports/2013/Teens-and-Tech/Summary-of-Findings.aspx>

"Teens and Illicit Drugs." *Pamf.org*. n.d. Web. 1 June 2013. <http://www.pamf.org/teen/parents/risk/drugs.html>

"Teens and Sex." *CanYouRel8.com*. June 2013. Web. 3 May 2013. <www.canyourel8.com/23>

"Teens and Young Adults." *AshaSexualHealth.org*. n.d. Web. 7 May 2013. <http://www.ashasexualhealth.org/sexual_health/teens-and-young-adults.html>

TeenGirlNow.com. n.d. Web. 13 Apr 2011. <http://teengirlnow.com/?s=relationship+survey>

Ulene, Valerie. "A Teen's Friends are a Powerful Influence." *LaTimes.com*. 11 Apr 2011. Web. 17 June 2013.

<http://articles.latimes.com/2011/apr/11/health/
la-he-the-md-teens-friends-20110411>

Wadley, Jared. "Decline in Teen Smoking Resumes in
2011." *Ns.umich.edu.* 14 Dec 2011. Web. 3 June 2013.
<http://www.ns.umich.edu/new/multimedia/videos/
20125-decline-in-teen-smoking-resumes-in-2011>

"What is Omegle? Is Omegle okay for kids?" *BeWeb-
Smart.com.* 20 Feb 2013. Web. 9 May 2013.
<http://www.bewebsmart.com/internet-safety/
what-is-omegle-is-it-okay-for-kids/>

Williams, Glenn. "What Can I Do if My Teen Is Using
Drugs?" *FamilyLife.com.* n.d. Web. 3 June 2013.
<http://www.familylife.com/articles/topics/
life-issues/challenges/addiction/
what-can-i-do-if-my-teen-is-using-drugs#.Ub6IOPlOOdc>

ABOUT THE AUTHOR

Shannon Perry is an author, conference speaker, national recording artist, and radio/television host. Shannon's television show called "Grace in High Heels" currently broadcasts into over 23 million homes via the NRB Network. Shannon also hosts a talk radio show on Salem Communication's KKHT Radio in Houston, Texas. Her first book entitled *Grace in High Heels: Real-life reflections of Humor, Hope and Healing* is based on one of Shannon's most popular women's conferences, "If The Shoe Fits." Before going into full-time ministry, Shannon spent over 14 years in the public school system as a teacher and school counselor. She holds a Master's Degree in Education and Counseling and is a Certified Instructor in Parenting Classes and Crisis Counseling.

As a recording artist, Shannon's latest CD was produced by Lifeway Christian Resources' Songwriter of the Year, Paul Marino. Shannon has performed at Carnegie Hall, with the Houston Symphony, and sang for over 70,000 fans at an NFL football game. Shannon is a contributing writer for *Believe.com* as well as *Crosswalk.com*, one of the most visited Christian sites on the web with over 24 million page views per month. She has contributed articles to magazines and e-zines such as *Charisma, Christian Voice, Christian Women of Today,* and *Everyday Christian,* among others.

For more information, visit
www.ShannonPerry.com.

MORE INSPIRATIONAL RESOURCES FROM SHANNON

Available BOOKS

"Grace in High Heels" is a short chapter book filled with Shannon's hilarious stories. Each chapter contains scripture, a powerful life-lesson and discussion questions. Perfect for use as a devotional tool or book study.

Available MUSIC CD's

"The Real Thing" includes songs written especially for each topic of *If the Shoe Fits*. Co-written with LifeWay writer/producer Paul Marino. Songs like *"Bad Hair Day"* and *"Keep On Pressing On"* garnered nationwide attention on radio. The song *"Long Way Home"* was written especially for Shannon's son Sean who serves in the United States Air Force.

Shannon's third CD, **"Tell the Story"** includes incredible music played by Grammy award winning musicians as well as songs that hit the national radio charts. Songs include *"Who's Gonna Love Me, God Is Doing*

Great Things, Tell the Story," and a song that Shannon sings especially for her dad entitled *"Love Never Ends."*

"Safe Place" is Shannon's sophomore project and includes seven original songs penned by Shannon including, *"David's Song,"* written for her husband, and *"Safe Place,"* one of the most requested songs that Shannon sings.

"Reflections," Shannon's freshman project, is a great variety of Southern Gospel and Light Contemporary. Songs like, *"Keep Walking On"* and *"Holy Ground"* are sure to lift your heart as you listen. Shannon sings, *"Thanks Again"* in honor of her mom and dad.

Available in AUDIO CD and DVD format
from the teaching series *If the Shoe Fits*

"Goody Two Shoes" emphasizes the importance of balance and knowing our purpose. Jesus never had a Franklin Planner or a Blackberry, yet He lived the most balanced life of any man who ever walked the face of the earth. Through humor and scripture, Shannon reminds us that we will live balanced lives when we know our purpose.

 In **"Lacing Up the Tongue,"** Shannon uses the practical illustration of a bridle along with scripture to remind us how we can heal or hurt those that we love the most by the words we speak. This session looks at seven different tongues we want to avoid if we are to tame our tongue for God's glory.

 Shannon shows us what scripture teaches about the promise of God's healing when we have been hurt in **"Is There a Hole in Your Sole."** Find out how to move forward into the amazing plans God has for us when we allow Him to have full control of the circumstances that hold us captive.

 Holiness—we hear it often in church, but what does Holiness look like in everyday life? In the session **"Walk A Mile In My Shoes,"** Shannon teaches the practical ways that we can live Holy lives, and reminds us of the blessings we will incur when we "walk a mile in HIS shoes."

To order these available resources,
visit the "Store" at www.ShannonPerry.com.

You may also contact us at
Chae Music 281-304-1278
or email sales@shannonperry.com

We want to hear from you! Please visit
Amazon.com and other on-line retailers to
write a customer review about

THE OVERLOOKED GENERATION